LÉON DI

HITLER FOR A 1000 YEARS

**TRANSLATED BY
ALEXANDER JACOB**

OSTARA PUBLICATIONS

LÉON DEGRELLE
HITLER
FOR A THOUSAND YEARS
Translated by
Alexander Jaocb

First published in French as
Hitler pour 1000 ans (Paris: La Table ronde. 1969).

This first English edition translated by Alexander Jacob
Published by Ostara Publications 2019
Ostarapublications.com
ISBN 978-1-64633-618-0

Contents

Preface — Alexander Jacob	1
Chapter I — The Muzzling of the Vanquished	7
Chapter II — When Europe was Fascist	14
Chapter III — Towards Power at the Age of Twenty Five	29
Chapter IV — Europe Explodes	42
Chapter V — Hitler, for a Thousand Years	67
Chapter VI — Alongside the Germans	77
Chapter VII — The Tramways of Moscow	86
Chapter VIII — The Russian inferno	97
Chapter IX — Who was Hitler?	119
Chapter X — From Stalingrad to San Sebastian	139
Chapter XI — The Exiled	153
Chapter XII — And if Hitler Had Won?	164
Select Bibliography — Degrelle's Post-war Writings	185

Preface

Alexander Jacob

Léon Degrelle (1906-1994) is today mostly remembered as the Belgian politician who founded the Rexist movement in Belgium during the thirties and volunteered as a soldier of the Walloon legion of the German Wehrmacht during the Second World War. However, Degrelle was also a prolific writer whose accounts of Germany's Russian campaign in particular are worthy contributions to the war literature of the last century.

Degrelle indeed began his career in Belgium as a Catholic journalist who worked for the conservative Catholic periodical *Christus Rex*. He was strongly attracted to Charles Maurras's Integralist movement in France and gradually moved into a confrontational position with regard to the centrist Catholics of Belgium. This led to his formation of his own 'Rexist' Party in 1935, which became increasingly influenced by Italian Fascist doctrines. Degrelle was, as a socialist, eager to help the working classes who had suffered under the brute materialist Communism and the bourgeois Socialism of the established Left. His desire to reach out to the common people was clearly evident in the large meetings that he carefully orchestrated during his political campaigns in the thirties. Rexism achieved major political gains in 1936, obtaining more than 11% of the vote, but had to contend with the Flemish 'Vlaams Nationaal Verbond', which championed an independent Flanders even though it supported a corporatist state just as the Rexist Party did.

Furthermore, Degrelle's steadfast efforts to expose the corruption of the Catholic Party caused the Belgian Cardinal Jozef-Ernst van Roey to proclaim that Rexism was a 'danger to the country and to the Church' and that Catholics should not vote for it. While Degrelle increased his Fascist style of rhetoric in his popular meetings, the lack of official Catholic backing for his 'Catholic' party was compounded by the Cardinal's support of Degrelle's rival Paul van Zeeland, who succeeded in defeating Degrelle in the 1937 Brussels by-election.

Degrelle then became more anti-Semitic in the articles he published in *Le pays réel*, the organ of the Rexist movement, and also established contacts with the Spanish Falangist leader José Antonio Primo de Rivera (1903-1936) and the Romanian Iron Guard's Corneliu Codreanu (1899-1938). However, by this time, even the National Socialists, who had been following Degrelle's movement carefully, began to lose interest in the political potential of Rexism within Belgium. And by the time of the 1939 national elections, the Rexist Party's performance had dwindled to insignificance.

When the Germans invaded Belgium in 1940, the Rexists were mostly in favour of the German presence in Belgium, even though they had earlier advertised a position of neutrality in the war. Consequently, along with various Communist groups, Rexists too were arrested in May 1940 as anti-national elements and imprisoned first in Belgium and later in France.

Degrelle was spared extreme persecution on account of the belief of the French that he may be useful in providing them information regarding Hitler. When he was freed in July 1940, Degrelle tended towards an increasing devotion to National Socialist ideals. Finally, when the Germans undertook their invasion of Russia in June 1941, he volunteered, as a mere corporal, in the German army in its fight against Communism. Many Flemish Belgians too volunteered in the Legion Flandern.

Degrelle demonstrated extraordinary courage during the war and was decorated with the Iron Cross in 1942. Degrelle's 'Légion Wallonie' was also transformed into the Wallonie Division of the SS in June 1943 but only after Degrelle had signed an agreement with Himmler that the Walloons, whose autonomy he had earlier insisted on, would eventually be incorporated into the Germanic Reich.[1] With the liberation of Belgium in September 1944, the Rexist Party was banned and, at the end of the Second World War, many of its members were imprisoned or executed.

However Degrelle had, in January 1944, been promoted Hauptsturmführer and decorated in Berlin by Hitler with the Knight's Cross of the Iron Cross.

In April 1944 he was promoted Sturmbannführer and in August of that year received, again directly from Hitler, the Knight's Cross of the Iron Cross with Oak Leaves. In November 1944 he was named Volksführer der Wallonen by Hitler. At the end of the war, in April 1945, Degrelle — whose SS Division Wallonie had been fighting in Pomerania in February 1945 — managed to get away to Norway, where he found a Heinkel in Oslo in which he was able to fly to Spain.

In Spain he succeeded in obtaining protection from persecution by Franco's government largely because the Belgian Foreign Minister Paul-Henri Spaak and Franco were not able to agree on the conditions under which Degrelle would be extradited to Belgium.

During his 'retirement' Degrelle maintained contact with other SS officers like Otto Skorzeny (1908-1975), who served as military adviser to Egyptian President Mohammed Naguib in 1953 as well as to President Juan Perón in Argentina before working for the Mossad too in 1963.

Degrelle also supported several neo-Fascist movements and nationalists like Jean-Marie Le Pen, who however discounted Degrelle's self-proclaimed importance as the principal representative of a European National Socialist movement.[2]

Degrelle wrote several works before, during and after the Second World War. In Spain he wrote, among other works, a detailed account of the Soviet campaign, *La Campagne de Russie 1941–1945* (1949), the present work *Hitler pour mille ans* (1969)

---

1 See Martin Conway, *Degrelle: Les années de collaboration 1940–1944*, Ottignies, 1994, pp.206ff.
2 *Ibid.*, p.304.

and an unfinished series of works on Hitler called *Le Siècle d'Hitler* (1986–) of which nine volumes were planned but only five have been published.

The present work gives the reader a good idea of Degrelle's idealistic personality as well as of his tenacity as a political activist. His unrelenting effort to cleanse the Church of its corrupt political affiliations reveals a certain lack of political pragmatism. His decision to join the German army in a volunteer Belgian division also betrays something of an inferiority complex since he professedly did so in order to prove to the Germans that the French Belgians were equal to the Germans in valour and should therefore be treated as such when the war ended. And there is no certainty that Degrelle himself would ever have the political power to obtain for Belgium full equality with Germany.

Degrelle's intellectual superficiality too may be detected in the fact that, when he makes a final assessment of the achievements of Hitler in the present work, he points mostly to all the scientific and material inventions that Hitler had initiated — as if these could not have been equally achieved under any other ideology than the Fascist.

In fact, Degrelle values Germany's scientific accomplishments so much that he declares that the 'modern world was born' on the day that Hitler fired the first rocket in 1939 from the Peenemünde Army Research Centre.

However, it must be pointed out that Degrelle does emphasise the soldierly quality that the Waffen SS cultivated among the different European peoples during the war and suggests that this might have had a salutary effect on the post-war political ethos if Hitler had won the war. This military character of Fascist rule would have, according to Degrelle, especially avoided the liberal excesses that democratic rule forced upon Europe in the sixties:

The life of the youth of all of Europe would have known another spirit and another sense than leading an existence of beatniks and protesters, rightly revolting against democratic regimes which do not offer them anything objective that could excite them, suffocating them on the contrary throughout the miserable post-war years.

Degrelle also extols Hitler as a great unifier of Europe, like Napoleon before him. But he does not note any of the important differences between these two European leaders, such as, for example, Napoleon's emancipation of the Jews and Hitler's persecution of them.³ Degrelle applauds the open border policy of the European Economic Community as a basis of European integration but, without a spiritual foundation, such as that of the Catholic Church — which he himself had become doubtful of after his conflicts with it — it is hard to see how the economic, technological and social networks of his envisaged Fascist Europe would have differed from those encouraged by the EEC and its successor, the European Union. Degrelle merely believes that the Reich would have been more 'heroic' in its character:

On the European peninsula which emerged in the west, after the deluge of the Third Reich, were built, nevertheless, the first counters, badly stocked, still not very stable, of a Common Market that is rather like a barter-house. Good. But a true Europe, raised by a heroic and revolutionary idea, built big, would have had quite another allure!

Yet, in spite of Degrelle's obvious lack of political acumen, the present work does provide a very gripping account of the horrors suffered by the German army and its supporting divisions during the Russian campaign. It also presents refreshing reminiscences of Degrelle's meetings with Hitler that highlight the latter's character as a military genius — and as a 'simple' person. Further, in spite of the youthful idealism that never seemed to have left Degrelle

---

3 Perhaps because of the adverse effects of his anti-Semitic articles in *Le pays réel*, Degrelle does not even briefly consider in the present work the anti-Jewish orientation of the Third Reich or examine the difference that a Europe without Jews such as the Hitlerian Europe would make to the spiritual, social and political constitution of the continent. Rather, he tended in the post-war years to merely repeat — especially in an embarrassing open *Lettre à Jean Paul, à propos de Auschwitz* published in 1979 — the dubious arguments of the so-called 'Holocaust Revisionists' that the mass-extermination of Jews in gas-chambers is a scientific impossibility and that the entire massacre was only a 'gigantic Hollywood racket'.

either in his political activities in Belgium before the war or in his soldierly travails during the war, he does finally emerge as a staunch European nationalist whose effort at joining forces with the National Socialists during the war was undoubtedly inspired by a desire to substitute democratic Liberalism and Communism with a more genuinely European, and pan-European, Fascist ethos. It may also be noted that, unlike Hitler and the National Socialists, Degrelle did not look down upon the Slavs, whom he considered to be endowed with a rich spiritual character that would complement the qualities of the western Europeans. As the champion of a merger of western Europe with the Slavic east, thus, Degrelle may be considered a forerunner of the other Belgian European nationalist, Jean Thiriart (1922–1992), who proposed a similar project of a unified Europe extending from the Atlantic to the Pacific that would be infused with a socialist concern for all Europeans and elevated by anti-liberal military virtues.[4]

---

4 See, for instance, Jean Thiriart, *The Great Nation: Unitarian Europe from Brest to Bucharest,* tr. Alexander Jacob, Melbourne: Manticore Press, 2018, and *Europe: An Empire of 400 Million Men,* tr. Alexander Jacob (Avatar Editions).

Chapter 1
The Muzzling of the Vanquished

What rights remain to us, survivors of the Eastern Front in 1945, overwhelmed by losses, consumed by pain? We are dead men. Dead men with legs, arms, breath, but dead men.

To pronounce a word in public, or write ten lines when one has fought, weapon in hand, against the Soviets and, above all, when one has been a so-called 'Fascist' leader is considered straightaway by the 'democratic' side as a provocation.

It is possible for a common bandit to explain himself. He killed his father? his mother? bankers? neighbours? He reoffended? Twenty international newspapers will open their columns to his memoirs, will publish the account of his crimes under snorting titles, ornamented with a thousand garish details, whether they are about Chessman[5] or about ten of his followers.

The clinical descriptions of a common assassin will be worth the printing — and the millions — of a bestseller like that of the punctilious analyst, the American Truman Capote.

Other mass murderers like Bonnie and Clyde will know the fame of the cinemas and will even dictate fashion in the poshest shopping centres.

As for the politically convicted, it depends. It's the colour of their party which will call for their justification or their execration.

---
5 Caryl Chessman (1921–60) was an American robber, kidnapper and rapist who was sentenced to death for crimes committed in 1948 in the Los Angeles area.

A 'campesino', a boorish peasant who became a team leader of the Frente Popular,[6] and who was never smothered by scruples when it was a matter of mowing down the ranks of the Nationalists, was able, in Spain itself, and in hundreds of thousands of copies, in the most widely circulated newspaper of Madrid, to explain, at great length and freely, what his adventure as a Spaniard of the 'Left' had been.

But, you see, he was of the Left.

So he had the right, just as all men of the Left have all the rights.

Whatever may have been the crimes, even the massive exterminations which the Marxist regimes culminated in, nobody will make them look glum, the conservative Right because it, quite foolishly, prides itself in being open to dialogue, the Left because it always covers its henchmen.

A revolutionary agitator like Régis Debray[7] will be able to count on all the listeners that he wants; hundred bourgeois newspapers will repeat his words with resonance. The Pope and General de Gaulle will rush to protect him, the one in his tiara and the other in his military cap.

How, in this context, not to find a parallel with Robert Brasillach, the greatest writer of France of the Second World War?[8] Passionate about his country, to which he had really devoted his work and his life, he was also mercilessly gunned down in Paris, on 6 February 1945, without a single military hat being moved, unless to give the signal to fire to the executionary squad . . .

Similarly, the Jewish anarchist born in Germany called Cohn-Bendit, perfunctorily searched for and, of course, never found by

---

6 The Frente Popular was a coalition of left-wing organisations established in 1936 which won the Spanish elections in 1936. The conservatives and monarchists mounted a coup d'état in July of that year provoking the Spanish Civil War (1936–39).

7 Régis Debray (1940–) is an academic and philosopher who associated with Che Guevara in 1967 and supported Salvador Allende in the seventies.

8 Robert Brasillach (1909–45) was a French author who supported the Fascist leaders of Europe including the Frechman Jacques Doriot and Léon Degrelle himself. He was executed in 1945 for his collaboration writings and activities.

the police of Paris when he had been quite close to blasting all of France, was able, whenever he wanted and as he wanted, to publish his studies, as incendiary as mediocre, in the capitalist publishing houses, pocketing while sniggering the checks that the latter offered him to cover his royalties!

The Soviets had perched their dictatorship on sixteen and a half million people murdered: to continue to commemorate the martyrdom of the latter would be considered as absolutely incongruous.

Khruschev, vulgar acrobat of the pig market, chickpea on his nose, sweating, dressed like a vendor of scraps, travelled triumphantly through the United States of America, with his old lady on his arm, escorted by ministers, billionaires, can-can dancers and the fine flower of the Kennedy clan, rewarding them, finally, with his boots damp socks on the table during a full session of the U.N.

Kosygin's badly baked potato head was offered the flowery homages of Frenchmen always disturbed by the evocation of Auschwitz but who have forgotten the thousands of Polish officers, *their allies of 1940,* that the USSR murdered methodically at Katyn.

Stalin himself, the worst killer of the century, the implacable total tyrant, having caused in his demented furore, his people, his collaborators, his military chiefs, his family, to be massacred, received a fabulous golden sceptre from the most conservative king in the world, the king of England, who did not even understand the macabre and comical aspect of the choice of such a gift to such a criminal. But if we, the 'fascist' survivors of the Second World War, had the impertinence to unclench our teeth for a single moment, at once thousand 'democrats' begin to yelp frenetically, frightening our friends themselvs who, supplicating, cry out to us, 'Be careful! Be careful!'

Be careful of what?

Was the cause of the Soviets venerable to such a degree? Throughout a quarter century, the world's spectators have had striking opportunities to become aware of its maleficence. The tragedy of Hungary, crushed by Soviet tanks in 1956, as expiation of the crime that they had committed of reviving a taste for freedom; Czechoslovakia levelled, muzzled by hundreds of thouands of Communist invaders, in 1968, because it had had the ingenuity of wishing to free itself a little from the horsecollar that Moscow had fastened around its neck, as around a Chinese convict; the long sigh of the peoples oppressed by the USSR, from the Gulf of Finland upto the shores of the Black Sea, show clearly what horror the whole of Europe would have known if Stalin had been able — and without the heroism of the soldiers of the Eastern Front he would have been — to get through to the quays of Cherbourg and the rock of Gibraltar.

From the inferno of Stalingrad (November 1942) to the inferno of Berlin (April 1945) nine hundred days passed, nine hundred days of fear, of battle every time more desperate, with horrible sufferings, at the cost of the life of several thousand young men who had had themselves crushed, ground, deliberately, for having tried to contain, in spite of everything, the Red armies hurtling from the Volga to western Europe.

In 1940, between the sudden burst of the Germans on the French border near Sedan and their arrival at the North Sea, there was a period of just one week. If the European combatants of the Eastern Front, among whom there were a half-million volunteers of twenty eight non-German countries, had hurtled with the same speed, if they had not opposed, inch by inch, in the course of three years of atrocious combats, an inhuman and superhuman resistance to the immense Soviet tide, Europe would have been lost, submerged without hope already at the end of 1943, or at the beginning of 1944, much before General Eisenhower had got his first apple-tree in Normandy.

A quarter century confirms that. All the European countries that the Soviets conquered, Estonia, Lithuania, Latvia, Poland, East Germany, Czechoslovakia, Hungary, Romania, Bulgaria remained, since then, implacably, under their domination. At the least disturbance, whether at Budapest or at Prague, it is the modern 'whip', that is to say, the Russian tanks cutting down the

The Muzzling of the Vanquished

recalcitrants at point-blank range. From July 1945, the westerners who had so imprudently gambled on Stalin began to become disillusioned. 'We have killed the wrong pig' murmured Churchill to President Truman at Potsdam, while they both left an interview with Stalin, the true winner of the Second World War.

Late and pitiable regrets . . .

The one who had seemed to them earlier to be the 'good pig' installed by them on two continents, grunted with satisfaction, his tail in Vladivostock, his snout fuming two hundred kilometres from French territory. The snout is still there, for a quarter century, more menacing than ever, to such a degree that nothing is dared at the present moment to affront it, other than a couple of kowtows.

On the day after the crushing of Prague, in the summer of 1968, the Johnsons, the de Gaulles, the Kissingers, confined themselves to Platonic protests, to fearful and reserved regrets.

In the meanwhile, under the belly of the above-mentioned pig, half of Europe is suffocated. That is not enough?

Is it right, is it decent that those who saw clearly in time, those who threw, from 1941 to 1945, their youth, their romantic liasons, their home, their strength, their interests on the bloody path of the Soviet armies, continue to be treated like pariahs, until their death and beyond death even? . . . Pariahs whose lips they seal as soon as they try to say, 'but nevertheless'.

Nevertheless . . . We had happy lives, houses where it was good to live, children that we cherished, goods that gave comfort to our lives . . .

Nevertheless . . . We were young, we had vibrant bodies, that were loved, we inhaled fresh air, spring, flowers, life with a triumphant avidity . . .

Nevertheless . . . We were inspited by a vocation, tending towards an ideal . . .

Nevertheless . . . We had to throw our twenty years, our thirty yeras and all our dreams into horrible sufferings, incessant anguishes, feel our bodies devoured by cold, our flesh torn by wounds, our bones broken in our bodies, in surreal bodies.

We saw our suffering comrades retch into the viscous mud or into the violet snow of their blood.

We emerged alive, well or ill, from these killings, distraught with fear, pain and torments.

A quarter century later, when our dear parents are dead in dungeons or have been murdered, and we ourselvers have arrived, in our distant exiles, at the end of our tether of courage, the vicious, vile 'democracies' continue to pursue us with an inextinguishable hatred.

Formerly, at Breda[9] — as one can see it still in the unforgettable painting of Velasquez in the Prado museum in Madrid — the victor offered his arms, his commiseration and his affection to the vanquished. A human gesture! To be vanquished, what a suffering already in itself! To have seen one's plans and efforts collapse, to remain there arms limp before a future that has been lost forever, of which one should nevertheless regard the empty frame in front of oneself, upto one's last breath!

What a punishment, if one had been guilty!

What an unjust pain if one had only dreamed of pure triumphs!

Now one understands that, in less ferocious times, the victor advanced in a fraternal manner, towards the vanquished, took in the immense secret pain of the one who, even if he had saved his life, had just lost all that gave it meaning and value . . .

What does life mean still for a painter whose eyes have been plucked out? For a sculptor whose arms have been broken?

What does it mean for the politician broken by destiny, and who had borne in himself, with faith, a burning ideal, who had possessed the will and the strength to transpose it into the facts and the life even of his people?

---

9 Breda is a city in the southern Netherlands. *La rendición de Breda* ("The Surrender of Breda") is a painting by the Spanish painter Diego Velázquez in 1635, depicts the exchange of the key of Breda from the Dutch defenders to the Spanish conquerors.

Never will it be realised, never will he create . . . For him the essential thing has stopped.

This 'essential thing' in the great tragedy of the Second World War, what was it for us?

How did the 'fascisms' — which have been the essential thing of our lives — arise? How were they deployed ? How did they collapse?

And, above all, after a quarter century: what balance sheet can one draw up of this whole gigantic affair?

Chapter II
When Europe Was Fascist

To a young boy of today the so-called 'fascist' Europe appears like a distant world, already confused.

This world has collaped. Thus it was not able to defend itself.

Those who dashed it down remained standing alone in 1945. They have, for a long time, interpreted the facts and the intentions as it suited them.

A quarter century after the debacle of 'fascist' Europe in Russia, even if there are some works that are half-correct on Mussolini, there is not yet a single obective book on Hitler.

Hundreds of works have been devoted to him, all botched or inspired by a visceral aversion.

But the world still awaits the balanced work which will establish the assessment of the life of the principal political person of the first half of the XX century.

The case of Hitler is not an isolated one. History, if one may say so, has been written since 1945 in a one-way direction.

In the half of the world dominated by the USSR and Red China it is not even thinkable that a writer who is not a conformist or an adulator would be allowed to express himself.

In western Europe, if the fanaticism is more nuanced, it is just more hypocritical. A major French or English or American newspaper would never publish a work that would highlight what might have been interesting, or creative in a healthy way, in Fascism or in National Socialism.

When Europe was Fascist

The very idea of such a publication would seem aberrant. One would at once cry out that it was a sacrilege.

One sector has been especially the object of passionate concerns: hundred reports, often exaggerated, sometimes grossly untruthful, have been published with a gigantic splash on the concentration camps and on the crematory ovens, the only elements that one takes care to consider well in the immense creation that was, for ten years, the Hitlerian regime.

Upto the end of the world, one will continue to evoke the death of Jews in the camps of Hitler under the frightened gaze of millions of readers, not very keen on exact counts or historical rigour.

Here also one waits for a serious work on what *really happened*, with figures verified methodically and cross-checked; an impartial work, not a work of propaganda; not things that are said to have been seen and that were not seen; not above all 'confessions' riddled with errors and nonsense, dictated by torturing officers — as a commission of the American senate had to recognise — to accused Germans playing for their head and ready to sign anything in order to escape the gallows.

These incoherent hotch-potches, historically inadmissible, have, without doubt, had an effect on the vast sentimental population. But it is the caricature of a distressing problem, and unfortunately as old as mankind.

The study is yet to be written — and besides, no publishing house will publish it! — which would exhibit the exact facts according to scientific methods, replace them within their political context, insert them honestly into a totality of historical connections, alas all indisputable — the treatment of the Negroes conducted in the course of the XVII and XVIII centuries by France and England, at the cost of three million African victims succumbing in the course of atrocious roundups and transfers: the extermination, through greed, of the Red Indians hunted down on the lands of the United States of today; the concentration camps of South Africa, where the Boers who were invaded were stationed like beasts by the English under the complacent eye of Mr. Churchill; the frightful executions of the Sipahis in India by the same servants of Her Gracious Majesty: the massacre by the Turks of more than a million Armenians: the liquidation of more than sixteen million non-Communists in the USSR; the charring by the Allies in 1945 of hundreds of thousands of women and children in the two most gigantic crematory ovens of history: Dresden and Hiroshima; the series of massacres of civil populations which have only continued and increased since 1945: in the Congo, Vietnam, Indonesia, Biafra.

One will wait for a longer time, believe me, before such a study, objective and of universal scope, will take stock of these problems and assess them without prejudice.

Even on much less burning topics any historical explanation still remains, at the moment, almost impossible, if one has had the misfortune of falling, politically, into the wrong side.

It is unpleasant to speak of oneself. But finally, of all the so-called 'fascist' leaders who took part in the Second World War, I am the only survivor. Mussolini was assassinated, and then hanged, Hitler shot a bullet into his head and was then burnt. Mussert, the Dutch leader, and Quisling, the Norwegian leader, were shot. Pierre Laval, after having undergone a short parody of justice, poisoned himself in his French jail. Saved with great difficulty from death, he was beaten ten minutes later and semi-paralysed. General Vlassov, the leader of the anti-Soviet Russians, delivered to Stalin by General Eisenhower, was hanged on a gallows in a Moscow square.

Even in exile, the last of those who escaped have been savagely pursued: the leader of the Croatian state, Anton Pavlevitch, was riddled with bullets in Argentina; I myself, hunted everywhere, escaped only by a millimetre from diverse attempts at liquidation by assassination or abduction.

Nevertheless I have not yet been eliminated at the moment. I live. I exist. That is to say, I could still bring forth a testimony capable of presenting a certain interest historically. I knew Hitler at close quarters, I know what human being he was *really*, what he thought, what he wanted, what he prepared, what his passions were, his moods, his preferences, his fantasies. I knew, in the same way, Mussolini, so different in his Latin impetuosity, his sarcasms, his effusions, his weaknesses, his urges, but he too extraordinarily interesting.

If objective historians still existed, I could be for them a very valuable witness with regard to their documents. Who, among the survivors of 1945, knew Hitler or Mussolini more directly than I? Who could explain with more precision than me, explain what type of men they were, men as they really were?

Nevertheless I really have only the right to be silent. Even in my own country.

That I would publish — twenty five years after the facts ! — in Belgium a work on what was my public action is quite simply unthinkable.

Now, I was before the wars the leader of the opposition in this country, the leader of the Rexist movement, a legal movement, adhering to the norms of universal suffrage, involving considerable numbers of politicians and hundreds of thousands of electors.

I led, during the four years of the Second World War, the Belgian volunteers of the Eastern Front, fifteen times more numerous than their compatriots fighting on the side of the English were. The heroism of my soldiers is indisputable. Thousands of them gave their life for Europe, certainly, but first of all and above all, to achieve the salvation of their country and prepare its resurrection.

However, there exists no possibility of explaining to the people of our country what the political action of Rex was before 1941 and its military action after 1941. *A law* prohibits me formally from publishing a single line on that in Belgium. It prohibits the sale, diffusion, transport of any text that I might write on these subjects! Democracy? Dialogue? For a quarter century the Belgians hears only one bell; as for the other — mine ! — the Belgian state turns on them all its cannons.

Elsewhere, it is not better. In France, my book *The Russian Campaign*, was hardly published before it was prohibited. It was the same, even recently, with my work *The Burning Souls*. This book is purely spiritual. Nevertheless it was officially put out of circulation in France, and that twenty years after my political life had been crushed!

It is thus not the ideas of the excommunicated themselves that are on the index but their names, which the democratic Inquisition relentlessly strikes down.

In Germany the same methods.

The publisher of my book *The Forgotten Legion* was, from the publication of the volume, the object of such threats that he himself had thousands of copies that were going to be distributed to booksellers destroyed some days after their release.

The record was beaten by Switzerland, where not only did the police confiscate thousands of copies of my book *La Cohue de 1940* two days after its publication but it rushed to the press and had the printing formes melted before its eyes in order that any reprinting of the work became materially impossible.

Now, the publisher was Swiss! The press was Swiss! And if some people considered themselves abused in the text it was easy for them to demand legal compensation from my publisher or from me. Which was of course nobody dared!

Same difficulties with speaking as with writing. I challenged the Belgian authorities concerned to let me explain myself before the people of my country at the Sports Hall of Brussels or to accept — nothing more! — that I present myself as a candidate at the parliamentary elections. The sovereign people would have decided. Could one have been more democratic? The minister of justice himself replied that I would be led *illico presto*[10] to the border if I disembarked at Brussels! To be absolutely sure that I would not reappear they improvised a special law, called Lex Degreliana, which prolonged by ten years my statutory period, which had expired ! So how could the crowds weigh the facts, the intentions, form an opinion? . . . And how, faced with such an imbroglio, could a young man discern the true from the false, the more so that the Europe before 1940 was not a single bloc? Each

---

10 immediately

country, on the contrary, presented very particular characteristics. And every 'fascism' had its own orientations.

Italian Fascism, for example, was very distinct from German National Socialism. Socially the German positions were more audacious. By contrast, Italian Fascism was not anti-Jewish essentially. It was rather more of a Christian tendency. And more conservative also. Hitler had liquidated the last vestiges of the empire of the Hohenzollerns whereas Mussolini, even if he did so grudgingly, continued to follow the feather-duster, half a metre tall, which moved its vast branches above the little toothless head of King Victor-Emmanuel.

Fascism would have been able to be as much against Hitler as with Hitler. Mussolini was, above all, a nationalist. After the murder of the Austrian chancellor Dollfuss in 1934, he had lined up several divisions at the border of the Reich. Deep within himself he did not like Hitler. He distrusted him.

'Be careful! Be careful of Ribbentrop above all!', he repeated to me twenty times.

The Rome-Berlin Axis was forged above all by the clumsiness, and the provocations, of a big press of the most suspect sort and of defeated and ambitious politicians such as Paul-Boncour,[11] the dishevelled clown of Paris, a nerveless and wilted Don Juan from the quays of Geneva, and such as Anthony Eden, the tall polished broom of London, and such as, above all, Churchill. I knew the latter, at the House of Commons at that time. He was very controversial and discredited there. Bitter when he had a dry stomach (which was, besides, very rare), his teeth clenched between his extremely fat bulldog jowls, one hardly paid attention to him. Only a war could offer him one final chance to accede to power. He clung stubbornly to this chance.

Mussolini, upto his assassination in April 1945, remained, deep down, anti-German and anti-Hitler, in spite of all the professions

---

11 Joseph Paul-Boncour (1873–1972) was a French socialist politician who served as Prime Minister of France from December 1932 to January 1933 and twice as Foreign Minister, in 1932 and in 1938.

of attachment that the latter poured out to him. With black eyes, as brilliant as black marble, his skull as smooth as the marble of baptismal fonts, the arched back of a fanfare leader, he was born to display his superiority. To tell the truth, Mussolini was enraged to see Hitler dispose of a better human instrument, the German people, disciplined, not asking for too many explanations, than that which was near them (the Italian people, charming, taking pleasure in criticism, fickle too, vibrant larks that are blown by the wind). From this bad temper there emerged secretly a strange inferiority complex that was increasingly aggravated by the victories of Hitler, who, until the end of 1943, always won in spite of the unheard-of risks that he took. Mussolini, on the contrary, an exceptional head of state, did not have the vocation of a war leader any more than a Romagnol country warden did.

In short, as men, Hitler and Mussolini were different. The German people and the Italian people were different.

As doctrines Fascism and National Socialism were different.

There were not lacking some points in common in the ideological field, as well as in action, but oppositions existed also, which the Rome-Berlin Axis reduced in the beginning but which the defeat that struck Italy in its blood and in its pride amplified and reinforced.

If the two principal 'fascist' movements of Europe, those even which were hoisted to power in Rome and Berlin, and which crossed the continent from Stettin to Palermo, seemed already so distinct one from the other, imagine the situation when one considers the other 'fascisms' that surged in Europe, whether in Holland or in Portugal, in Romania, Norway or elsewhere!

The Romanian 'fascism' was essentially almost mystical. Its leader, Codreanu, entered on horseback, dressed in white, to the large assemblies of Romanian crowds. His appearance seemed almost supernatural. It was, to such a degree that he was called the 'Archangel'. The militant elite of his members bore the name, the Iron Guard. The name was hard just as the circumstances of combat and the methods of action were. The feathers of the Archangel were peppered with dynamite.

By contrast, the 'fascism' of Portugal was dispassionate, as was its mentor, Professor Salazar, a cerebral person who did not drink, did not smoke, who lived in a monastic cell, was dressed like a clergyman, established the points of his doctrine and the stages of his action as coldly as if he were writing a commentary on the *Pandectes*.[12]

In Norway, it was yet another matter. Quisling was as happy as as an undertaker. I see him still, his face swollen, his eyes gloomy, dark, when, as Prime Minister, he received me in his palace in Oslo, at the end of a court of honour where a king, of bronze that had become green like a badly cooked cabbage, bore, high and proudly, a forehead covered with bird droppings. Quisling, in spite of his stuffy allure of a chief accountant dissatisfied with his cash, was as military as Salazar was not. He depended on militias whose boots were clearly more brilliant than the doctrine.

Even in England there were 'fascists', those of Oswald Mosley.

At the opposite end of the proletarian 'fascists' of the Third Reich, the English fascists were, for the most part, aristocratic fascists. Their meetings resembled the thousands of members of the gentry, come to see what those distant and fabulous phenomena that were called 'workers' might be (there were however some of them in Mosley's group).

The audience were multicoloured with the lively and conspicuous colours of young elegant people, moulded tight in fine silk robes; the container and the content vibrated with charm. Very exciting and very appetising, this fascism! especially in a country where the long thin poles of the feminine world reminded one so often of hop plantations!

Mosley had invited me to dine in a disused theatre, perched on the Thames, where he received his guests behind a white wooden table. It was very austere and very monastic at first glance. But perfect valets quickly appeared and the vessel in which they served you was golden!

---

12 The *Pandectes* are the compilation of Roman laws made by the Emperor Justinian in the sixth century.

Beside the proletarian Hitler, the theatrical Mussolini, the professorial Salazar, Mosley was the paladin of a rather fantastic fascism which, as extraordinary as it may seem, was consonant with British manners. The strictest Englishman cares about displaying very personal specialities, whether they be political or sartorial. Mosley presented another of these, as Byron or Brummel presented others formerly, and as the Beatles would offer others much later.

Churchill himself took care to distinguish himself in his manner, receiving imporant visitors completely naked, in the stuffed majesty of an anglicised King Bacchus, draped only in the smoke of his havanas. The son of Roosevelt, envoy to London on mission during the war, thought he would die of suffocation when he saw the Adam-like Churchill advancing towards him, his stomach puffed, fat as an obese innkeeper who has just washed his arse in a zinc tub on Saturday evening.

At the extreme opposite, the Mosley of before 1940, the impeccable fascist, covered in a grey bowler hat instead of in a steel helmet, armed with a silk umbrella instead of a truncheon, did not especially fall out of line with British eccentricity.

But nevertheless the fact that the English, solemn as ministerial porters and conservative as the Rolls Royce cars, allowed themselves, they too, to be intoxicated by the liquor of European fascisms before 1940 indicates to what point the phenomenon corresponded in Europe to the state of a generalised mood.

For the first time since the French Revolution, in spite of the diversity of nationalisms, burning ideas and a burning ideal provoked rather identical reactions.

One single faith sprang forth at the same time from one end of the old continent to the other, whether it was at Budapest, Bucharest, Amsterdam, Oslo, Athens, Lisbon, Warsaw, London, Madrid, Brussels or Paris.

In Paris, not only did the fascist spurts possess their own characteristics but, besides, they were decomposed into multiple subdivisions: of dogmatic tendency, with Charles Maurras, the bearded old man, courageous, integral, deaf as a debtor, intellectual father of all the European fascisms but limiting his own, jealously, to the French territory; of military tendency, with the old soldiers of 1914–1918, moving, resounding, without ideas; of 'middle class' tendency, with the Fire Cross of Colonel de La Rocque,[13] who adored multiplying the large manœuvres and barrack inspections with civilians; of proletarian tendency, with the Parti Populaire Français of Jacques Doriot,[14] the old 'commie' in spectacles, acting voluntarily in his propaganda with his large shoes, his suspenders, his wife's kitchen apron, to appear working class, a class that remained recalcitrant to him as a whole after a rather successful beginning; of activist tendency and smelling of gunpowder, with the balaclava of Eugène Deloncle[15] and Joseph Darnand,[16] the hard ones, the dynamic, who dynamited with delight, in the middle of Paris, the unfeeling offices of the super-capitalists, in order to blast them in a flash out of their golden sleep.

Deloncle, a very intelligent polytechnician, would be cut down by the Germans of 1943 and Joseph Darnand by the French of 1945, even though he had been one of the most fearless heroes of the two world wars.

This overabundance of Parisian 'fascist' movements theoretically parallel and practically rivals, divided and disorganised the French elites. It would end on the evening of 6 February 1934, in the bloody riots of the Place de la Concorde in Paris, though power, fallen in the slippery panic, was not caught by the hands of a single one of the victors of the 'Right'.

---

13 François de la Rocque (1885–1946) was the French leader of the right-wing league, Croix de Feu (Fire Cross) from 1930 to 1936.
14 Jacques Doriot (1898–1945) was a French politician who began as a Communist but became the leader of the Parti Populaire Français which championed Italian Fascism as well as German National Socialism.
15 Eugène Deloncle (1890–1944) was the leader of the Organisation Secrète d'Action Révolutionnaire which undertook terrorist attacks against left-wing activists in France. Deloncle was assassinated by the Gestapo in 1944 for his collaboration with Wilhelm Canaris and other members of the Abwehr (German Military Intelligence Service) who were opposed to Hitler.
16 Joseph Darnand (1897–1945) was a collaborator of the Vichy regime who participated in the terrorist activities of the secret group 'La Cagoule'. In 1943 he became a Sturmführer (lieutenant) of the Waffen SS.

Their great man of that night was called Jean Chiappe,[17] police prefect of Paris, dismissed three days earlier by the Leftist government.

He was a voluble, blushing Corsican, bearing a rosette of the Legion of Honour in the form of a tomato, quite small in spite of superimposed soles that made one think, when he spoke to us, that he was perched on a barrel. Even conducting himself like a spring cherry tree, he felt his sides, took care of himself; suffering rheumatism, he said, he did not even go out on 6 February with the demonstrators. He had just taken a hot bath and was preparing to go to bed, in pyjamas. In spite of the increasingly insistent and then panicking reprimands of those loyal to him, he refused to dress, when he would only have had to cross the road to sit in the empty armchair of the Elysée!

In 1958, General de Gaulle, facing the same armchair, would not need to be begged so much!

Between these multiple French 'fascist' parties the common denominator before 1940 was a weak one.

In Spain, General Primo de Rivera[18] had, before many others, been a 'fascist' in his way, a monarchist 'fascist' a little like Mussolini. This concession to the throne contributed much to his failure. Too many palace courtiers, specialists in tripping people up, slippery as eels, deep as hoses, lay in wait for him. Too few proletarians supported him, proletarians of simple heart, with strong arms, who could have also followed a Primo de Rivera harnessed to the social reform of his country rather than fall into line behind the *pistoleros* and the incendiaries of the Frente Popular. The court intriguers caused this experiment to get stuck in the glue of the prejudices of a socialite aristocracy, vain and politically sterile for several centuries.

---

17 Jean Chiappe (1878–1940) was a right-wing civil servant who served as Préfet de Police in the thirties.
18 Miguel Primo de Rivera (1870–1930) was a Spanish general who headed a military dictatorship from 1923 to 1925. He sought to return to civil government between 1925 and 1930 but lost the support of the army and was forced to resign in January 1930.

José-Antonio,[19] the son of the general, who was ousted and dead in Paris some days later, was an inspired orator. He had understood, in spite of his heredity as a *senorito*,[20] that the essential thing of political combat of his time resided in socialism. His programme, his ethics, his personal power could have rallied millions of Spanish people to him who dreamed of a renewal of their country, not only in greatness and in order but also, and especially, in social justice.

Unfortunately for him, the Frente Popular had mined the terrain everywhere, misled the masses, raised between the Spaniards the barricades of hatred, fire and blood. José-Antonio could have been the young Mussolini of Spain in 1936. This tall splendid boy saw his dream ruined in that very year by an execution squad in Alicante. His ideas marked his country for a long time. They inspired hundreds of thousands of combatants and militants. They rebounded, revivified by the heroes of the Division Azul, even upto the bloody snows of the Russian Front, bringing their part to the creation of the new Europe of that time.

We see that the Spain of 1939 was not the Germany of 1939.

Not any more than Colonel de La Rocque in Paris, stiff as a metronome with a colourless mind like a macadamised road, was not the spitting image of Dr. Goebbels, lively as a photographer's flash; not any more than Oswald Mosley, the refined fascist of London was the *alter ego* of the fat Dr. Ley[21] of Berlin, violet like a barrel of new wine.

However, the same dynamism worked on the crowds everywhere, the same faith raised them, and even a rather similar ideological foundation was noted among all of them. They had in common the same reactions towards the old sclerotic parties corrupted in sordid compromises, deprived of imagination, not having brought social

---

19 José Antonio Primo de Rivera (1903–36) was the son of Miguel Primo de Rivera and founder of the Fascist 'Falange Española'. He was arrested and executed in 1936 by the Frente Popular. However, he was regarded as a martyr during the Francoist regime.
20 The Primo de Rivera's were aristocrats, Miguel the second Marquess of Estella and José Antonio the third.
21 Robert Ley (1890–1945) was the National Socialist leader of the Deutsche Arbeitsfront (German Labour Front).

solutions anywhere that were vast and truly revolutionary, whereas the people, overwhelmed with hours of work, paid miserably (six pesetas a day under the Frente Popular!), without sufficient protection against industrial accidents, sickness, old age, waited impatiently and anxiously to be finally treated humanely, not only materially but also morally.

I shall always remember the dialogue that I heard, at that time, in a coal mine that the King of the Belgians had entered:

What do you want? asked the sovereign, rather awkwardly, filled with the best intentions, of an old miner black with soot.

Sir, replied the latter, First of all, what we want is that we are respected!

This respect of the people and this will to social justice was allied, in the ideal 'fascist', to the will to restore order in the state and continuity in the service of the nation.

A need to raise oneself spiritually also. Across the entire continent the youth rejected the mediocrity of the professional politicians, small-minded wastrels, without education, culture, electorally supported by cabarets and by the dressed-up semi-notables with wives who had married too young, were badly loved, overtaken by events and who cut down the least idea or least boldness of their husbands with the broad strokes of a pruning shear.

This youth wanted to live for something great, pure.

'Fascism' emerged everywhere in Europe spontaneously, in very diverse forms, from this vital, total and general need for renovation: renovation of the state, strong, authoritarian, having time for itself and the possibility of being surrounded by competent people, avoiding the vagaries of political anarchy; renovation of society, detached from the suffocating conservatism of the gloved and hard-necked bourgeois, without perspective, flushed with excessively rich food and excessively rich Burgundy, intellectually closed, sentimentally and especially financially, to every idea of reform; social renovation, or more exactly social revolution, liquidating paternalism, so dear to the rich who played lightly with calculated tremolos on the hearts and preferred to the recognition of legal rights the condescending distribution of limited and supported charities; social revolution, relegating capital to its place as a material instrument, the people, the living substance, becoming once again the essential basis, the primordial element, of the life of the fatherland; moral renovation, finally, in teaching the nation, the youth especially, to raise itself up and look after itself.

There is not one European country which, between 1930 and 1940, did not hear this call.

The latter presented distinct nuances, distinct orientations, but it possessed, politically, socially, quite similar bases, which explains that, quickly, an astonishing solidarity was built up: the 'fascist' Frenchman went, anxiously at first but very soon with enthusiasm, to help the processions of the 'Brown Shirts' in Nuremberg; the Portuguese sang the 'Giovinezza'[22] of the Balillas,[23] just as the Sevillans sang the 'Lili Marleen' of the Germans of the North.

In my country, the phenomenon arose, as elsewhere, with its own characteristics, the unificatory elements that had emerged from the Second World War in the different European countries styled in the course of a few years. I was, at that time, a very young boy. On the back of a photo I had written (I was modest):

'Here more or less true, the features of my face. The paper does not express the burning and proud fire which burns in me today, which burned in me yesterday. And which tomorrow will burst like a storm.'

The storm I bore in myself. But who else knew it? Abroad, nobody knew me. I had the sacred fire, but had at my disposal no support which could suddenly assure me of a great success. However, a single year was enough to gather hundreds of thousands of disciples, to shatter the somnolent tranquillity of the old parties and to send to the Belgian parliament, in one blow, thirty one of my young comrades.

---

22 'Giovinezza' was the hymn of the Italian Fascist Party and national anthem between 1924 and 1943.
23 The Opera Nazionale Balilla was the Italian Fascist youth organisation.

The name Rex, would be revealed in a few weeks, in the spring of 1936, to the whole word. I arrived at the shores of power even at the age of twenty nine, at the age when normally boys take an apéritif on a terrace and caress the fingers of a pretty girl with glowing eyes. A wonderful time, when our fathers did not have to do anything more than follow us, when, everywhere, young people, with wolves' eyes, with wolves' teeth, stood up, leaped, arrived, prepared to change the world !

Chapter III
Towards Power at the Age of Twenty-Five

At twenty eight, I saw my life as a political leader breaking into a thousand pieces and my military life (general, commander of an army corps) shatter.

How, at twenty five, could one force oneself through the life of a state and arrive at the threshold of power so quickly and so soon?

Success depends on the epoch and this is the proof. There are some who ooze with boredom and suffocate every vocation. There are others in whom what is exceptional surges and grows and deploys itself. Bonaparte, born fifty years earlier, would doubtless have terminated his career as a paunchy mayor in a provincial city.

Hitler, without the First World War, would doubtless have vegetated as a bitter semi-bourgeois in Munich or Linz. And Mussolini would have remained a primary school teacher in Romagna all his life, or moved to the prison of Mamertino Prison, an impenitent plotter in the sleepy centuries of the Pontifical States. The spiritual and passionate currents as well as the examples that inspired Europe around the 1930s opened exceptional horizons to vocations and ambitions. Everything was in ferment.

Everything exploded: the Turkey of Ataturk — an impressive giant of health, partied the night like a drunkard, exercising during the day an omnipotent authority, the only dictator who had the luck to die in time, that is to say, in his bed — as well as the Italy which Mussolini had just taken control of. A motorised Caesar. The Duce had in a few years turned an anarchist and weary country into an orderly country. If I was Italian, I would be a fascist, shouted Winston Churchill once.

He repeated this same affirmation to me one evening at table in London, at the restaurant of the House of Commons.

And yet, Italy irritated him, which had dared to move from the modest role which the Powers had assigned to it to that of an imperial country reserved upto then exclusively to the British gluttony and pride.

More than anything else, the example of Mussolini had fascinated Europe and the world.

He was photographed naked to the waist cutting wheat in the dried Pontins marshes. His planes crossed the Atlantic in impeccable squadrons. An Englishwoman had rushed to Rome, not to shout out a hysterical love for him, like so many others, but to discharge on it, not very nicely, a bullet which missed him by a hair's breadth. His young Balillas parading everywhere and singing. His workers inaugurated impressive social installations, the most lively on the continent, at this time. The Italian trains no longer stopped right in the middle of fields, as in 1920, to oblige the curate to descend who had had the nerve to stand in front of it! Order reigned. And life. Everything progressed. Without bets being shouted out. And without social fracas.

Industrialised Italy was born, from ENI to Fiat, where Agnelli created, on the orders of the Duce, a popular car much before he left with the Italian volunteers for the Russian Front, in 1941, where he fought alongside us in the Donets basin.

This industrialised Italy which made its international debut after Mussolini was dead, it was — one forgets it too often — Mussolini who created it.

His great African empire was going to extend in some years from Tripoli to Addis-Ababa, Mussolini not letting himself be intimidated by the international protests of hypocritical countries that had gorged first and did not tolerate the idea that poor countries would have the insolence to expand or, at least, to eat when hungry without having to allow hundred thousand or two hundred thousand empty stomachs emigrate wretchedly every year towards the ghettos of Brooklyn or towards the fevers of the South American pampas.

In each country, thousands of Europeans considered Mussolini, studied Fascism, admired its order, the panache, élan, the important political and social accomplishments.

One should do the same! they repeated nodding their head. Numberless discontented people, and especially an entire youth thirsty for ideals and action, aspired to be raised by someone in their turn, as Mussolini had done in his fatherland.

Even in Germany, the Italian example did not fail to help the victory of Hitler. Of course, Hitler, was self-sufficient. He possessed a wonderful sense of crowds and action, a striking courage. He risked his life every day. He struck out. He threw out elemental key ideas. He inflamed the masses that became more and more vehement. He was cunning, and at the same time, an extraordinary organiser.

Hitler's father was already dead very early on, one morning, struck down by apoplexy, falling head first into the sawdust of a café. His mother was dead, of tuberculosis, a few years later. At sixteen he was an orphan. Nobody helped him any more. He had to force himself through. He was not even a German citizen. He was nevertheless going to become in twelve years the leader of the most important party of the Reich, and then its chancellor.

In 1933, he was the master, he had raised himself to power, democratically, let us emphasise, approved by the absolute majority of German citizens and by a parliament elected according to democratic norms, where Christian Democrats and Socialists would approve, by a positive vote, their confidence in his nascent government.

Increasingly impressive referendums would reaffirm this popular support. And these referendums were sincere. People have claimed the contrary, later. This is materially false. In the Sarre, a German province upto then occupied by the Allies, who had installed themselves there from the autumn of 1918, the referendum was organised and supervised by foreign delegates, and supported by foreign troops. Hitler was not even authorised to put in an appearance in this region during the electoral campaign. However, he obtained in the Sarre exactly the same triumphal vote (more than twenty four percent of the votes) as in the rest of Germany. Identical proportions were repeated from Danzig to Memel, German towns, also controlled by foreigners.

Fact is fact: the immense majority of Germans were either lined up behind Hitler already before his victory or else had, in an unceasingly growing enthusiasm, rallied their troops, as millions of ex-Socialists and ex-Communists had done, convinced of the benefits of his dynamism.

He had returned millions of unemployed back to work. He had injected a new strength into all the sectors of economic life. He had reestablished social and political order everywhere, a masculine order, but also a happy order. The pride of being a German radiated throughout the Reich. Patriotism had ceased to be a defect, it was deployed like a glorious standard.

To claim the contrary and affirm that Hitler was not followed by his people is to grossly deform the state of mind then and to deny the evidence of the facts.

At the extreme opposite, and exactly at the same time, the Spain of the Frente Popular stunned the foreign observer by its absurd violences and its sterility. Much before losing the war militarily, the *Frente Popular* had, in Spain, lost the war *socially*. The people did not see any gun-shots fired at the more or less marked out bourgeois or plump curates, nor at Carmelite skeletons that were exhumed to expose them on the Alcala street.

The Frente Popular had been incapable — and that was, however, what mattered — of creating in Spain even the outline of a social reform. One cannot repeat enough to the young Spanish workers: their fathers, from 1931 to 1936, did not know anything else, under their Red leaders, — among the shots of assassinations and the conflagrations of convents — than scandalously miserable salaries, instability of employment, insecurity in the face of illness, accident, old age.

The Frente Popular should have — that was the one-time opportunity of proving that the politicians of the Left defended the people! — given to working Spain salaries that would have permitted them to live, social insurances which would have guaranteed their existence, threatened by capitalist selfishness, by strikes and by crises, which would have assured the family of the worker security in the case of accident or of death.

Socially, the Frente Popular was a bloody zero. In 1936, its social and political failure with regard to the powerful, always growing social accomplishments of Fascism and of Hitler, were strikingly evident to all objective viewers.

It could only put into greater relief the benefits of the formulas of political and social order, the faults of Communist and Socialist demagogic formulas, whether it was in a Moscow crushed — and unceasingly purged — by Stalin or in the anarchy of Madrid, where the Frente Popular succeeded, with the cowardice of rabbits, in abducting the leader of the opposition, the member of parliament, Calvo Sotelo, in the middle of the night and in having him assassinated by its policemen with machine-guns.

In this atmosphere, the crisis could only accelerate into the heart of every country of Europe. It helped me, it is certain, to plant in an instant my banner on the ramparts of the old political citadel in my country, decrepit as it was at that time in all the countries of the continent.

Of course, I also, I was born for combat.

Opportunity, circumstances helped. They clear the terrain but they are not enough. One must possess political flair, the sense of action, jump over opportunities, invent, renew one's own tactics in the course of one's march, never have fear of anything and, above all, be burning with an ideal that nothing stops.

Never, in the course of my entire public activity, did I doubt, for one second, my final success. Anyone who would have expressed the least reservation to this proposition in front of me would have astonished me.

Did I at least have extraordinary collaborations or imposing means ?

In no way. Absolutely not. I had not been pushed forward by any personality, even of second rank. I achieved my great electoral triumph in 1936 having fished for candidates no matter where, without financial aid of any leader or any economic grouping.

I was born deep in the Belgian Ardennes, in a small village of less than three thousand inhabitants. We lived in a tight circle, my parents, good provincial bourgeois, and with seven brothers and sisters in the vale of our mountains. Family life. The river. The forests. The fields.

At fifteen, I entered the Jesuit college at Namur. Already at that time I wrote. And also I spoke sometimes in public. But how many other people write or speak ! At twenty, a student in law and political science, at the University of Louvain, I had published some books. I published a weekly newspaper. My papers were read. But, finally, all that was still somewhat normal.

But the start accelerated.

I took over a publishing house of the Catholic Action which was called REX (Christus Rex) whence was born the weekly REX, which would in two years reach a circulation truly fabulous for Belgium of that time : 240,000 copies sold, of each issue.

I should have been able to manage. To launch a large political movement across a country seemed to everybody like an enterprise that demands many millions. I did not possess any money, it was quite simple.

I had begun by publishing out of the blue brochures that were related to every event that was somewhat sensational.

I edited their text in one night. I launched them in a flashy way, like a brand of soap or sardines, with imposing, paid, advertisements in the mainstream press. I had, very rapidly, mounted a team of fourteen motorised propagandists (free motorbikes, compensated with publicity in my first publications). They traversed the entire country, pushed my brochures onto the leaders of scholarly institutions who loved to pocket considerable commissions by entrusting the diffusion of my papers to their kids. The drivers of my roaring cars were paid also, solely according to the number of their sales. My brochures reached approval through very high circulations: never less than 100,000 copies; and even once 700,000 copies.

So that went well.

When my weekly REX appeared, I had already had, in addition to my motorised agents, numerous groups of determined propagandists. They called themselves Rexists. They undertook the great conquest of the public, posted everywhere at the entrances of churches and cinemas. Each centre of propaganda of REX lived on its discounts and supported, thanks to them, all its expenses. Soon our press was a source of considerable income, covering all the disbursements of our activities.

One can say that the brilliant development of REX came about thanks to a press written in a dynamic fashion and sold in a dynamic fashion, paid for by the readers, who themselves completely financed the great breakthrough of Rexism.

Our combat obliged me suddenly to create a daily, the *Pays réel*. I had ten thousand francs at my disposal. Not a cent more. With which to pay the third of the edition of the first day. I had to work like a galley slave. I myself wrote the essential part of the newspaper in impossible conditions. My copy represented the equivalent of a volume of three hundred pages every fortnight.

But the daily penetrated the market, reached, after our victory, a sensational circulation: in October 1936, more than 200,000 copies on a daily average, verified by a bailiff's declaration every night.

But the political conquest of a country must be able to depend on *spoken words* as well as on *writings*. One had never seen a political movement in Belgium, or elsewher, reunite readers without its costing the organisers very dearly. Now, to dispose of such sums, or even much less sums, was materially impossible. I therefore had to reach audiences as I had reached readers, wihtout any expense. I searched for the public, which would not cost me anything.

In Marxist meetings debates were offered in their advertisements even though nothing was ever presented to this end, everybody saving his skin and his integrity. I went there punctually. Every evening I was there.

It's Leon! murmured the crowd. Everybody, soon a considerable public, knew me. And the fights unleashed to enervate me helped me powerfully, echoed by the press. My bones, apart from a cranial fracture in 1934, had remained remarkably intact. In the meanwhile, our propagandists, enflamed by their ideal, excited by this direct action and by these risks, had become thousands: the most ardent boys, the most beautiful and well formed girls. Rex appeal, the King Leopold would say.

I could then mount my own meetings. Meetings which, from the first day, were paid ones. That had never been seen, but I considered that good. Up to the last evening of the electoral campaigns the Belgian audience paid five francs every evening to hear me. The explanation had been clear: a hall costs so much, the publicity so much, the heating so much, the lighting so much, total so much, each pays his share, that is clear and correct.

In this way I gave several thousands of meetings several every evening, of two hours each time, or more, always argumentative. One day I spoke fourteen times, from seven in the morning to three in the morning of the following night.

I chose the biggest halls, such as the Sports Palce in Anvers (35,000 seats) and the Sports Palace in Brussels (25,000 seats). More than 100,000 francs in entry tickets every time! I gave there also six large meetings six days in a row that I called the Six Days, since I beat the record in the biggest cyclist enclosure of Belgium: 800,000 francs in entry tickets!

I rented disused factories. I mounted, in open air, in Lombeck, at the gates of Brussels, a meeting where more than 60,000 listeners came: 325,000 francs in entry tickets!

This money was not so important. Never, as the leader of REX, did I touch a cent of the pay. The money was valuable as a means of action. But we possessed in this way, everywhere, at no cost, a second and formidable means of action.

Imagination did the rest. Our propagandists painted the bridges, the trees, the routs. They even painted entire herds of cows which displayed on their flanks along the railway lines, the three enormous red letters of REX, putting the train passengers in a good mood, enchanted by the surprise of the spectacle.

In a year, without any support whatsoever, through force of determination, sacrifices, and faith, we had, with some thousand young boys and young girls, revolutionised the whole of Belgium. In their electoral prognostics the old politicians did not grant a single winner to us, we had suddenly thirty one! Some were real boys. The one that shocked the minister of Justice, at Renaix, was just old enough to vote at that time ! The proof had been made that, with will and especially when a powerful ideal pushes you forward, anything can be established and anything can be won. Victory is to those who wish and to whose who believe.

I say that to encourage the young, ardent, who might doubt their success. But in reality the one who doubts if he will succeed cannot succeed. The one who must force Fate carries in himself unknown strengths that perspicacious and tenacious scholars will certainly discover one day but which have nothing in common with the physical and psychic machinery of the normal being.

'If I were a man like others, I would now be drinking a jug of beer in the market café', Hitler had replied to me one day when I recounted to him, in my mocking tone, that the genius is normally abnormal.

Neither was Mussolini a 'normal' being. Napoleon had not been that before him. When the abnornal strengths that sustained him abandoned him, his public life fell to the ground, like an eagle whose two wings had been suddenly cut.

Mussolini, during the last year of his life — it was visible and tragic — floated like a disoriented raft on a sea that would absorb him at any time. When the mortal wave appeared, he welcomed it without resistance. His life was finished when the unknown forces which had made him Mussolini had ceased to be his secret blood.

Secret blood. That's it. The others have common blood, analysed and catalogued. They become, when they succeed, generals like Gamelin,[24] knowing all the strings of the general staff and drawing correctly, or politicians with a false collar like Poincaré, meticulous, applied and orderly like tax-collectors. They did not break anything. Normal humanty ends, in its upper levels, as enthusiasts, whether it be about the state, the army, or the impeccable construction of skyscrapers, of a highway or a computer. Below these normal minds that are distinguished are the immense herd of normal beings who are not distinguished. Humanity is they: some thousands of human beings of average intellect, average heart, average routine.

And then suddenly one day the sky of a country is crossed by the great shining lightning of the being who is not like the others, of whom one does not yet know really what he has that is exceptional. This lightning reaches, among the immense crowd, forces of the same origin as his own, but atrophied and which, receiving the issuing shock, are revived, respond, correspond, on a small scale, feeling their life transformed nevertheless. They are animated, elevated by fluids that had never reached their normal life and which they had never suspected would penetrate their existence.

A genius is this formidable emitting and absorbing rod, whether he be called Alexander or Genghis Khan, Mahomed or Luther, Victor Hugo or Adolf Hitler. Geniuses, leaders of people, the geniuses, magicians with colours, volumes or words, are projected, to more or less intense degrees, towards ineluctable destinies.

Some fools are also, doubtless, geniuses, geniuses who have gone out of control, whose mysterious power an error must have distorted, or badly joined together, at the start. In fact, scientists, doctors, psychologists as yet know next to nothing of this nature of genius. But a genius is not made, he is not the result of enormous work, he comes under the category of a physical or psychic state

---

24 General Maurice Gamelin (1872–1958) was the general who commanded the French army during the disastrous Battle of France in May–June 1940.

that is still unknown at present, a special case which is produced as one in ten thousand, or a million or hundred million. Whence the amazement of the public. And the grotesque aspect of judgements made by banal beings on the extraordinary beings who excel them in everything.

When I hear simpletons express with confidence Olympian judgements on Hitler, or even on Van Gogh or Beethoven, or on Baudelaire, I sometimes wish to snort with laughter.

What do they understand ?

They miss the essential thing, because they do not possess actively this mysterious power which is the essence of genius, whether of the complete genius with maximum high voltage or the limited genius, because his expansive power is less charged, less rich or he is oriented towards a limited sector.

The genius, good or bad, is, whether one wishes or not, the yeast of the heavy and monotonous human dough. The latter would fall flat on itself without this stimulant. This yeast is indispensable. And Nature has it only sparingly. And it is necessary that the circumstances are present that permit these molecules of superior life to ferment uniform nature, thousand times more considerable, materially, but which, left to itself, is vain, vegetates, and represents nothing.

Without the genius who, from time to time, pierces it, the world would be a world of civil servants. Only the genius causes the universe to come out sometimes from its mediocrity and surpass it. The lightning extinguishes itself, it falls into the greyness from which only a new lightning can perhaps make it resurge one day.

That is why the epoch of fascisms from which authentic geniuses emerged was captivating. Among the exceptional circumstances transformers of peoples of exceptional radiance emerged. The world was, on account of them, going to know one of the most extraordinary turns in its history.

Did everything turn out badly?

What do we know?

At the fall of Napoleon, one thought that everything had turned out badly. And yet, Napoleon has left his mark on humanity forever. Without Hitler, would we be even at the threshold of the exploitation of the atom? Would there have existed a single rocket? Now the radical change of our epoch starts from these.

The discharge of the genius of Hitler, if it — and there is a whole complex that should be analysed — provoked catastrophes, certainly also brought forth a radical transformation of the orientation of humanity. The new universe that emerged from the Hitlerian drama provoked in a few years an irreversible change in the conditions of life, of the behaviour of the individuals of society, of science and economics, of the methods and techniques of production, changes that are more considerable than all those which the last five centuries brought forth.

Hitler was perhaps only the dynamite cartridge that triggered the gigantic explosion of our time and provoked the upheaval of the contemporary world. But the upheaval took place. Without Hitler, we would have remained, perhaps for hundreds of years more, the same petty bourgeois civil servants that we were in the first quarter of the century.

From 1935, the ignition of the Hitler satellite was inevitable. Genius is not stopped, during the countdown every country was going to participate in its way and often unconsciously in this fantastic upheaval, some acting as negative poles — France and the British Empire, for example — others constituting positive poles, each of them joining together pieces of the machinery from which would emerge the future world.

But in 1936 which soothsayer would have imagined that the aged world in which he lived was going to experience such a total change? Hitler, rumbling with unknown forces that constituted his real life, was he himself aware of the destiny that awaited him, and which awaited us all?

I, like the others, still saw only that my people had to be extracted from the political swamp, morally as well as materially. In 1936, the country, the fatherland were still, everywhere, the alpha and omega of every citizen. A French prime minister like Pierre Laval[25] had never spent a single day of his life in Belgium, two hundred kilometres from Paris! Mussolini had never seen the North Sea. Salazar did not know the colour of the Baltic Sea.

I indeed travelled in Asia, Africa, Latin America. I had lived in Canada, in the United States. But I hardly spoke of it, for that did not seem serious enough, smacking almost of restlessness.

In fact, the international spirit, and even the European spirit, did not exist. The only international organism, the League of Nations, in Geneva, was a useless gossipy old woman of whom men of polite society spoke with condescendance. It had gathered together, over twenty years, the principal European statesmen. A Briand[26] had vaguely had a glimpse of Europe there. And yet his conception of it was very blurred. But his case was almost the only one. Europe, without Hitler, would have remained there, doubtless for a long time yet, each country acting within the fields of its particular territory.

In less than three years, the old continent was going to suffer a total transfomration. Before it could even blink its eyes, the Hitlerian mushroom, grandiose, frightening, would unfold over Europe. The particles would invade every corner of the sky, upto the most distant depths of the oceans.

---

25 Pierre Laval (1883–1945) was a French politician who served (1931–32) as Prime Minister during the Third Republic as well as as head of government (1942–44) in Marshal Pétain's Vichy government. He was arrested in 1944 for collaboration with the enemy and executed the following year.

26 Aristide Briand (1862–1932) was Prime Minister of France during the Third Republic (between 1909 and 1929). During the interwar period he signed the Locarno Treaties with the German Foreign Minister Gustav Stresemann and authored, along with the US Secretary of State Frank Kellogg, the Kellogg-Briand Pact of 1928 which renounced militarism as a means of resolution of disputes between its signatories.

Chapter IV
Europe Explodes

If you had taken power in time in Belgium would you have been able to prevent the Second World War ?

At first glance the question seems quite absurd, for Belgium is a handkerchief thrown to the side in the north-west of the continent. Its 30,000 km² represents little. And the interests at play, both from the Germano-Italian and from the Franco-English side, were gigantic. So ? . . .

Well, this 'so ?' is not as problematic as it might appear at first glance. Between the two blocs of western Europe which were going to grapple with each other the only country capable of constituting a barrier or a meeting place of two great rivals was still Belgium.

Positioned at the top of the state, disposing of the only means of international propaganda that radio was at that time, it would have been possible, attached to the microphone every day, to oppose, during the France of the Front Populaire, the violent belligerent campaigns that sought to set Paris definitively against the Third Reich.

The French polemicists were just a minority. A very small minority. They were seen during the Munich Agreement in September 1938, after which the French signatory, the minister Daladier, an honest cultivated drunkard, who expected to be hit with rotten tomatoes and eggs on disembarking at the Bouret airport, was acclaimed by the Parisian 'people' with a frenzy which left him stuttering and flabbergasted. He is there even during the war of Poland. The Frenchman, in spite of the customary gulps of

Europe Explodes

wine, takes to arms reluctantly. He fought badly in 1940, not only because Hitler's strategy excelled his general staff, clumsy and a century old, but because he did not understand anything of the aims of this war and was lacking in morale.

Informed daily, from 1936, the French people would perhaps have understood the problem of the reunification of a Reich fragmented foolishly after 1918. The have a bright mind. Politically they choose that which is reasonable. They would have been able to realise that the best would be for *themselves* to propose, in time, a total regulation, on just grounds, of the problem of the German borders, and notably of Danzig, a city separated arbitrarily from the Reich, which voted 99% for Hitler and which, in the name of 'democracy', was forbidden to rejoin the fatherland of its history, race, langauage, and *preference*.

So, what was the use of the right of peoples to dispose of themselves ?

On the other hand, Danzig was the strait through which the maritime life of the new Poland passed.

It was impossible, evidently, that a large country like Germany would remain forever cut into two, that its inhabitants would continue to be unable to come together except in lead-sealed wagons, across a foreign territory.

Poland for its part had the right to breathe, to extend its windpipe upto the Baltic. Nevertheless, this imbroglio of the Polish Corridor was not a remedy.

The solution of a friendly Polish-German plebiscite was relatively simple, which would have guaranteed to each of the two countries that it would be either the victor or that it would be defeated in the electoral competition, with either a free access by means of a highway unifying the two parts of the Reich if the Germans lost or connecting Poland to the Baltic Sea if the Germans won.

The search for a similar or fairly similar, or even a different, solution but one satisfying the parites concerned was certainly easier to develop than the plans of cohabitation imposed in 1919 on very different peoples, rivals sometimes, enemies often: the millions of Czechs, Slovaks, Ruthenians, Hungarians on the old Bohemian buffer zone; on millions of Poles, Ukrainians, Jews and Germans in the heart of a hybrid Poland without a national majority. Or on a Yugoslavia of Croats, Serbs and Bulgarians who hated one another, who dreamed more of tearing one another apart than of embracing.

But, you see, it was not necessary, in order to envisage a solution pertinent to the case of the Danzig corridor, to wait until one had come to 30 August 1939, when the engines of some thousand tanks already growled through East Prussia from Pomerania to Silesia!

France gave striking evidence of its diplomatic skill before 1914 by solving the Anglo-French intimacies, by tying the Franco-Russian knot; it renewed them under de Gaulle by dissociating itself from the politics of blocs. The same skill would have been equally able in 1936 to help prepare a peaceful solution of the German puzzle.

And then the Hitler of 1936 was not the roaring Hitler of 1939. I met him at length at this time, for the interest of my country, a land in between, was to establish intelligent and precise relations with the leaders of the European game. It was in this way that I saw discreetly all the principle statesmen of Europe, whether they were French, like Tardieu and Laval, or Italian, like Mussolini and Ciano, or German, like Hitler, Ribbentrop and Goebbels, or Spanish, like Franco and Serrano Suñer[27] or English, like Churchill and Samuel Hoare.

In August 1936 I had met Hitler at length. The meeting had been excellent.

He was calm and strong. I was twenty nine years old and very bold.

---

27 Ramón Serrano Suñer (1901–2003) was a Spanish politician who served as Interior Minister and Foreign Affairs Minister in Franco's government between 1938 and 1942. It was he who suggested that the Division Azul of Spanish volunteers join the Wehrmacht on the Russian Front.

'I have never seen such gifts in a boy of this age', Hitler had repeated to Ribbentrop and Otto Abetz after our interview. I quote this judgement not in order to deck myself in peacock feathers but so that one may see that the personal chemistry had worked, that the conversation that I had held with him for several hours, with Ribbentrop present, had interested him.

Now, what had I proposed? Nothing more nor less than a meeting of Léopold with Hitler at Eupen-Malmedy, another territory separated from Germany by the Treaty of Versailles, for the benefit of Belgium this time, after a rigged referendum: those who were not in agreement had been obliged to make their opposition in writing by affixing their signature on a public register, a formidable directory of future suspects!

In these conditions who would have signed?

All the bells of Belgium rang in vain to celebrate this so-called annexation! In the long term such procedures were indefensible. In my opinion, it was necessary to prevent claims and bury the axe of war especially where there was a possibility of brandishing it.

Hitler was in agreement with my formula immediately: a referendum whose prepatory campaign would be limited to an assembly of local populations in front of two state leaders who would be present together and explain publicly their point of view, with complete courtesy; a second identical assembly would be held after the referendum in order that, whatever the result may be, the two state leaders would ratify the reconciliation of their two peoples.

If Hitler rallied to such a peaceful solution — which pleased Léopold III too when I went to share it with him — he could have accepted, with greater reason, in 1936, a debate concerning all the borders, Austrian, Czech, Danish, etc., and notably an amicable arrangement with a Poland reconciled since 1933 with the Reich and friend, on the other hand, of a France which would have been, on this occasion, the ideal agent of a definitive regulation.

A little before, Marshal Pétain and Marshal Goering had met, in Poland itself. Nothing sensible was therefore impossible.

There were no statesmen who had not deplored, from 1920, the foolishness of the decisions taken, following the First World War, on the subject of Danzig, the Corridor and Silesia.

The decisions imposed then had been unjust, based on dictates and rigged referendums.

Studied calmly, a wise solution should have been present much before it was a question of the Anschluss and the Sudetens, so much more since the atmosphere, in Poland as in Germany, was for collaboration, to such a point that, when President Hacha, repudiated by the Slovaks, had entrusted on 15 March 1939 the fate of Bohemia to Hitler, the Poland of Colonel Beck participated militarily in the investment, taking control of the town and the region of Teschen. Such a Poland, well advised, would have refused with difficulty a serious debate with its ally, of that very spring.

Without the provocative intervention of the English at the end of April 1939, promising the moon to Colonel Beck, a physically and financially crazy man, this agreement would have been negotiable.

The appeals to the spirit of understanding of the French would have been decisive. Hitler had publicly and forever renounced Alsace-Lorraine. He did not in any way wish to cross swords with an unassimilable France, that is to say, without any interest for a conqueror.

France, for its part, had nothing to gain from such a trifle. The more the fecund lands of the east could have tempted Hitler — and one should have even oriented and encouraged him in this direction, freeing the west, for hundred years, from the German danger — the more would a war, sterile from the start, with France have ceased to awaken in him the least desire.

A Belgian government leader, the son, grandson and great-grandson of Frenchmen, explaining to the French the vital importance of their role as mediators, as I would have done unceasingly planted before the microphones of the radio broadcasts, would have been able to impress the minds of the French.

In any case, I would have attempted the impossible.

I would have been annoyed to death for not having seized power in time, even if it offered me only a minimal chance to save the peace. I would have used it to the maximum. The passion of achieving that would have dictated the words that were necessary. The French people is sensitive to verbal orchestrations. And it was ripe for the language that I would have offered it.

The most astonishing thing is that, if I was not able to seize in time in my strong hands a power that I would never again, believe me, have relinquished, the goal escaped me precisely because of Hitler. It was the interventions pushed through in Austria, among the Sudetens, the Czechs, then the beginning of the Polish fight, which frightened the Belgian public and jeopardised my final ascension. Which does not prevent my having been depicted thousand times, at that time, as being the instrument of Hitler, the plaything of Hitler. I have never been the plaything of anybody, not of Hitler any more than of any other, not even during the war when I fought on the side of the German armies on the Eastern Front. The most secret archives of the Third Reich establish this. Neither in 1936 nor later, nor ever, did I receive a penny or a payment from Hitler. Never, besides, did he try to inluence me in anything.

On the contrary, later, when the political uncertainties of the war distressed me, I told him some amazing things about it. His chief translator, Dr. Schmidt, who was present as an interpreter during our interviews, himself recounted, in the press, after the war, how I spoke to the Führer with a vigour and a crudity that nobody else had ever dared to use with such an interlocutor.

He put up with it very well, with a good sense of humour.

'Léon', he told me during the war, when I demanded everything from him for my country and refused everything in its name, 'finally it is not you who collaborate with me, it's I who collaborate with you!'

And that was true.

Our country, because too small, risked losing its personality in a badly defined Europe. I always demanded that the actual character of our people be respected in everything: its unity, its customs, its faith, its two languages, its national hymn, its flags. I never tolerated, all through the long campaign in Russia, that a German, as sympathetic as he might have been, would exercise command amongst my units, or even just speak to us in German. We had to first assert ourselves. After that we would see.

Even with Hitler I held my conversations only in French (which Hitler did not know), which gave me, between outselves, the time to reflect well while the answer was being translated, though it was already understood. Hitler was not easily duped.

'Fox!', he told me one day laughing, after having detected in my eye a malicious look. But he was not offended by my subterfuges and allowed me to carefully weigh each of my remarks.

In 1936, in any case, we had not yet come to that point. Hitler was still for us a distant German. The era of the great operations of Germanic regroupment had not yet begun. The reoccupation of the left bank of the Rhine, logical, and which should have been conceded to the Germans a long time before, had not especially caused any misfortunes. It had been rapidly assigned to the balance of profits and losses.

At the moment of the victory of Rex (May 1936), the barometer of Europe was rather at fine weather. During our electoral campaign the name of Hitelr had not been evoked a single time by an opponent. One had confined oneself, in all the Belgian parties in the fray, to problems of internal politics.

Our programme of that time — the texts yellowed by time still exist — speaks at length and harshly of the scope of the old political paties, of the reform of the state (authority, responsibility, duration), of the socialism that was to be established, of the high finance to be subdued. But there is no question there of any sketch of an international programme.

For long months yet after our victory of 1936, our position was limited to advocating a politics of neutrality which would detach our country from every dangerous alliance — did de Gaulle act differently, later, faced with the two 'blocs' of the post-war period ? — and would maintain our fatherland apart from the quarrels that had begun to growl between the democracies of the old style (France, England) and the democracies of the new order (Germany, Italy). Under our impetus this politics of neutrality became rapidly — and officially — that of Belgium.

There was in all that, therefore, nothing that expressed an international orientation of Rexism in a pro-Hitlerian direction. Some great reforms of National Socialism and of Fascism interested us acutely. But we examined them as observers, nothing more.

To tell the truth, my affinities were French. My family was from there. My wife was from there and had conserved her nationality. My children could opt one day for the country of their choice. They have, since that time, all opted for France. From 1936 to 1941 I went only one time to Berlin but hundred times to Paris!

Also, there was no question of a German hand, German money, German orders! We were neutral. Neither with Germany nor with France: the most rigorous neutrality in the face of fight where our country had nothing to gain and where, between the two combatants agitated by violence, it could only receive bad blows, from both.

In any case, in the spring of 1936, such an altercation had not yet become the order of the day in Europe. We knew some weeks of respite. Then, during the summer, the avalanche crashed down.

First, in France, the Front Populaire won in the elections. Power passed to the leader of the coalition of the Left. Léon Blum, an enemy through his Marxist convictions as through his Judaism, of everything that was Hitlerian. His hostility and the blindness that hostility lends were such that he had predicted the failure of Hitler just before the latter came to power!

A series of ministers of his team, men and women, were equally Jewish. One cannot say that their passion for France was exaggerated: one of them, a bespectacled Mephisto called Jean Zay, had even, formerly, treated the French flag as toilet paper. But their anti-Hitlerian passion was, fanatic, without limits. Tension mounted immediately. The campaigns of anti-Hitlerian hatred and provocation, under such impulses, spread rapidly and effectively.

Supported deeply by the Hebrew propaganda, the Front Populaire rushed against anybody, abroad as well as in France, who was of the Right. I was described in its press just because I was a neutralist, as an accomplice of Hitler. It caused the secret agents of the French Second Bureau to act against me who were extremely numerous and active in Belgium, where they abundantly poured corrupting millions into the press and the social circles that had been fleeced and avid for pocket money.

A month later, the second electric shock: nationalist Spain rose against the Frente Popular, the dear brother of the French Front Populaire.

Spain and Belgium, not being neighbours, did not and could not have opposed interests in anything. The reaction was just, healthy, necessary, as the Spanish episcopate and then the Vatican were going to proclaim it the same year. Civil war is the last resort, but the furores of the Frente Popular had forced nationalist Spain to its last resort.

The Phalange, with a Catholic basis, was very close to Rexism, politically and spiritually. I myself had been named, in 1934, by José Antonio Primo de Rivera, the leader of the Phalange abroad.

The Spanish army that had risen up defended the same patriotic and moral ideas as those of Rexism.

And then, anyway! If the French Front Populaire, if the Soviets, if all the Marxist International, supported incendiaries and stranglers, if they frenetically supported them, if they heaped French aeroplanes and Russian tanks on them, if they sent them thousands of recruits — intellectuals like Malraux, bloody butchers like Marty,[28] or prison dregs — why could we, patriots and Christians, not have felt sympathies for the patriots and Christians hunted and persecuted for five centuries by terror and reduced to take up arms in order to survive? . . .

---

28 André Marty (1886–1956) was a French Communist who served as Politica Commisar of the Sovietic International Brigades operating from Albacete. His ruthless method of executing members suspected of disloyalty earned him the nickname 'the Butcher of Albacete'.

Europe Explodes

In any case, a first firebox of the European war had been lit. No firefighter appeared who would have been able to douse the nascent blaze. On the contrary, the fire expanded. Germans and Italian, Russian Communists and Red Frenchmen, moved from verbal exchanges to exchanges of explosives, aimed at using the Spanish battlefield to regulate their disputes with the sword.

Internationally 1936 ended badly. Nerves were highly strung, 1937 was going to mark, in Europe, the fatal curve.

From that time, Hitler, who had hardly to worry about the electoral plans of Rexism, was going to regularly keep an eye on us every time that we had to reinforce our activism by gaining new votes and with their help hoist ourselves peacefully to power.

It was, for me, a clearly limited position: no access to power through violence. Never, in times of peace, did I carry any weapons. One could see me in Brussels, or anywhere, without protection of any sort. I went to mass, to the restaurant or the cinema with my wife: she was my sole shield, full of graciousness and kindness.

I travelled kilometres into the woods with my children. I I have always felt a physical horror of everything connected with janissaires or bodyguards. I always believed in my star. Nothing will happen to me. And, in any case, a pistol in a trouser pocket would be pulled out too late and would not prevent the damage.

The people are horrified of these protections which betray suspicion. One should trust them, frankly. I went all alone by tram to the worst Red meetings. Incidents were not lacking. They were often comical. But my method was the best. The heart of the people is upright. One should appeal to their sentiments of hospitality and not to any noxious intimidation.

Just as I wanted to win the masses through their heart, without having recourse to a display of force, my entire being was opposed to a recourse to armed force to raise myself to power in my country.

This armed force I had at my disposal; in October 1936, the most famous and most popular leader of the Belgian army, General Chardonne, placed, in writing, all his troops at my disposal, offered to bring them in special trains to Brussels. The terrain would have been cleaned in an hour by the elite division that the Chasseurs ardennais were. The king — his secretary explained to the writer Pierre Daye, a Rexist member of parliament — had ordered that there should be no retaliation.

I thanked the general, but refused such an operation.

Without any doubt, if I had been able to guess how the international events were going to catch me off guard, I would have accepted. There would have been little resistance among the wealthy. Once I had taken a decision I would have had, in any case, smashed all obstacles wihtout ceremony: the salvation of my country and the peace of Europe would have had more value in my eyes than the screeching of some Marxist leaders, promptly locked up. But I was, deep down, sure of succeeding without recourse to a solution using force. My preferred solution was freely and enthusiastically consented conviction, adhesion and dedication.

At twenty nine, immense crowds had given themselves to my cause. Some months later, the Flemish nationalist leaders had rallied to my conception of a federal Belgium. Their members of parliament and senators, almost as numerous as mine, had formed a bloc with Rexism.

Why would this peaceful progress not be led without violence upto definitive victory? One more election, two elections, some powerful popular campaigns and I would arrive at power wihout the firing of a shot, supporting myself on the adhesion and affection of the absolute majority of my cocmpatriots!

But I failed to achieve that.

If I did not achieve that it is especially and above all, I repeat, on account of Hitler, who had moved from the era of the internal restoration of the Reich to the era of international claims, pushing the panic-stricken voters in all our countries under the umbrellas of the old conservative governments. At the beginning of 1937, the fight had been frightfully aggravated in Europe, kindled in an increasingly violent manner by the unceasing bravados of the French Front Populaire. Hitler responded to his enemies by dumping on them the loudest imprecations, the most cruel sarcasms, the most direct threats.

In six months, Europe found itself divided into two camps. Not that it ranged itself in this way: *it was ranged*. We who had no connection, no order at all, either political or financial, with the Third Reich, were thrown into the German clan, like a bundle onto a railway platform, where however we did not wish to land up at any cost.

I still hear, at the end of a meeting of the Left, during the winter of 1936–1937, the shout: 'To Berlin!' It was a total calumny. Nevertheless, I returned, anxious, to my friends who were present. 'Bad, that shout'. The following day, the entire Marxist press reported it. Henceforth, we were classified, in spite of our unceasing protests, as the men of Berlin!

But the supreme catastrophe was that Hitler, furious of the campaigns conducted everywhere against him, had begun to lose patience, to shout, to dig in!

And, every time, his rush, whether it was towards the Austrian Danube, or towards the mountains of the Sudetenland, or towards the beautiful baroque bridges of Prague, fell, always, as if automatically, right in the middle of the electoral campaigns of Rex, which could have brought the Belgian public behind us in a definitive manner.

Belgium — and that is understandable — had retained a horrible memory of the invasion of 1914, which had been as unjust as cruel. Each military outbreak of the New Germany into a neighbouring country, even if this enty had been peaceful, even if it had been accepted, or welcomed with enthusiasm as in Austria, threw the Belgian voters into a panic.

'To Berlin! To Berlin!' yelled the propandists of the extreme Left at us in chorus, sure of the effect of the slogan. To throw this calumny at our face in a cowardly way was to throw the voters, Walloon as well as Flemish, into a panic with total impunity. 'To Berlin!', when the Berlin in question, through its violent international moves, invariably flung panic, at the decisive moment, into the public that we were desperately trying to conquer. When I provoked the Belgian prime minister, M. Van Zeeland,[29] in 1937, to an actual referendum-election in Brussels, the shout 'To Berlin!' was unleashed throughout the campaign. It ended with a formidable blow that the archbishop of Malines dealt me, more anti-Hitlerian even than Léon Blum and all the Jewish committees combined.

Cardinal Van Roey was a colossal Flemish peasant built like a flint-axe, 'taciturn', stubborn, bearing under his attire strong tenacious odours. Some of his followers who admired him only partially had nicknamed him 'the rhinoceros'. Timid, the League for the Protection of Animals had not protested.

His archepiscopal palace, oppressively dull, was haunted by hunchbacks, squint-eyed people, cripples, lugubrious and silent lackeys bought at the lowest price. In front of the principal stairwary of waxed wood, diverse poultry cackled — 'My chickens', the archbishop murmured lugubriously, to all appearances not thinking of evil.

These were the only audiences at which he was present.

With an eternally sullen air he gave evidence in everything of a basic integral fanatism, as if he had dominated tribunals of the Inquisition and stakes in the XVI century. He had never read a single copy of a non-Catholic newspaper.

Even to think of it filled him with horror, and rendered his muddled face even more sullen. For him, a non-believer did not bear the least interest. To ask oneself questions on what an atheist might think would not even have come to his mind. The non-believer was, in his conception of the universe, a completely unusual being, an abnormality.

---

29 Paul van Zeeland (1893–1973) was a Belgian politician who served as Prime Minister and Minister of Foreign Affairs between 1935 and 1937. In the election of 1937 van Zeeland, representing the liberal Catholics and the working class, won against Degrelle, who accused him of accepting financial contributions from the national bank. When this was in fact confirmed by the investigation assigned by the government to the Finance Minister, Henri de Man, van Zeeland decided to resign in 1937, even though the contribution itself was not deemed illegal.

He led his archepiscopal troop as a sergeant major of Frederick the Great would have led his recalcitrant recruits to their exercices. He pushed away with his sacred shoe everything that did not have a glazed look, half-closed eyes, a nose bent downward like a banana, of the lay brother who threw himself on his knees, arms crossed, before the table of his superior, at the least lack of discipline. Today one would put him, stuffed and at first deodorised, in a post-conciliar museum. But at that time he ruled.

Apart from the problem of his marble impassibility towards non-believers which, spiritually, seemed to me to be a caricature and monstrous, we had, he and I, an egg to peel, as big as if it had been laid by an ostrich, an ostrich with golden eggs.

Regarding a question of millions of francs pinched from the Belgian state I had embarassed His Eminence to the highest degree by unmasking — among twenty others — the financial political scandal in which an ignoble little bank-shark named Philips, a crimson gnome with an enormous nose topped with a violet wart granulated like a berry, had wallowed for a long time and perfectly complacently,

This Philips irrigated generously (six million francs in 1934) the soutaned hierarchy that constituted the framework of the propaganda network of his bank. He was so much more generous since, thanks to the corruption of the Catholic party in power, he had caused the states (the Socialist colleagues had had at the same time similar subsidies adjudicated in favour of their collapsing Workers' Bank) to grant him astronomical financial 'subsidies'. I had uncovered the brigandage. I had dragged the 'banksters' by their feet to the middle of their trash, making them swirl in this rubbish in front of the whole of Belgium.

Philips could not do otherwise than pursue me before the tribunals. I had won. With great sweeps of the broom I had removed him from the political life of Belgium, throwing him literally out of the doors of the senate. He found himself there on the pavement with his dishonour, his wart turned purple and the vigorous mark of my boots on his old trembling buttocks.

'Living shit!' I had shouted to him, in front of the crowd, showing him the door. Now, this pick-pocket was, very ostensibly, the ward and the protector of the primate cardinal of Belgium. As mentioned, if I may be allowed a certain freedom of expression, apart from the archbishops, they were thick as thieves. The cardinal who did not smile at anybody, smiled at this hideous scoundrel as if at an angelic apparition.

Their intimacy was such that the archbishop, a homelover, had slept elsewhere in his honour, spending a weekend at the sumptuous castle that the banker had granted himself in a gracious Brabantine valley. I had photos of the two comrades walking piously under the bower, without one being able to tell very clearly if they were reciting some Biblical psalms together or if they were discussing less seraphically the increasing percentages of bishoprics turned into deaneries.

Some years earlier, when this banker was, politically, unknown, the cardinal Van Roey had give the order to the Catholic parliamentarians to coopt him as a senator, in place of an eminent intellectual of the Right, Firmin van den Bossche, who had already been chosen.

After that, to grab this Philips by the bottom of his trousers, defenestrate him and catapult him into the air until he fell, on his stomach, among his useless millions, was evidently somewhat profane! My crime did not have a name. All the fires of heaven would not suffice to make me expiate my impious solution.

Actring with the height of impudence, I did not stop with this disrespectful treatment of the debasements of the chosen, of those anointed by His Eminence. I had dealt with my boots, with the same sacred fervour, some dozens of colleagues of the above-mentioned senator, all equally hypocritical, always having the air of transporting the Holy Sacrament when they moved, pillagers and degenerates, among the cutthroats of high finance.

I had targeted, among the foremost, shooting point-blank right in the face of the president of the Catholic party, the minister of the interior, Paul Segers, a little boastful sacristan, always crowing, with the livid head of a cockroach who, between two prayers, had abundantly exploited the state bank and notably the bank of the small people, the Savings Bank.

On the part of the leader of these great Catholic bourgeois so satisfied with their high morality such a hypocrisy was particularly dishonourable. They were the typical representatives of a rotten elite that blatantly played at high virtue. I rushed at the Segers in question. I broke into the tribunal where he presided, the annual assembly of his party. It was — gods sometimes have a sense of humour — 2 November, the Day of the Dead.

I had brought with me three hundred chums who were ready for everything. The minister Segers, between his four palm-trees of the offcial tribunal, was treated by me for half an hour like a by-product of compound manure.

That was the greatest scandal in Belgium before 1940.

Like Philips, and with the same good fortune, Segers hailed me before the tribunals, demanding three million francs from me in damages and interests, destined to repair his 'honour'. Repair? What honour? These scoundrels of political finance, what did they have left that, indirectly or directly, could have still had some relation to honour?

The trial took place. Not only was I triumphantly acquitted (and God knows if I did not know anything at that time of the 'arrangements' of Justice!) but Segers, minister though he was, was condemned like a common swindler.

'You are the flag of the Catholic party' a senator called Struye, with the bust of a suburban hairdresser mounted with the head of a bespectacled toad, had shouted to him, on the eve of the trial. The said toad, after the Liberation, touched by a delayed vocation as slaughter-house butcher, would get revenge for the condemnation of his 'flag' by sending a more than hundred of our comrades to the gallows.

The case of Belgian democracy before 1940 was the case of all the democratic governments of that time, weak, that is to say, open to all temptations. Every one of them knew the scandals of that time: Barmat[30] in Germany, Stavisky[31] in France (both Jews, it may be said in passing).

But the police took care every time to resolve the bad affair with remarkable speed. Barmat had been found, very early in the morning, dead in his cell and Stavisky, on another early morning, had had himself killed at point–blank range by the cops who had surrounded his villa in Chamonix at night. They freed in this way from all worries the French financial horde and as compensation lived off his plunders.

In Belgium — and nobody will ever forgive me for this — I had not saved the Staviskys, Walloon or Flemish, and had not permitted them to be saved. On the contrary, I had maintained their dirty rotten heads under the water until the last bubble of air had surfaced.

But every time that I got rid of a shady politician who disguised himself with the name 'Catholic' — which seemed to me more scandalous than everything else! — my new crime was inscribed in the black book of the cardinal.

It was, however, he, good God, who should have thrown them out of the glass windows of the cathedrals!

But no, the guilty person was me who, broom in hand, hunted down, as a sincere Catholic, the crooks of political finance, crouched behind the confessionals and the fonts!

The cardinal had intervened, in December 1936, to the Vatican, to obtain a condemnation of Rexism. He had failed. Crouched behind his cripples, his hunchbacks and his cross-eyed people of the Archbishop's palace, he watched out for me. He waited for the right time.

---

30 Julius Barmat, and his brother Henri, were Russian Jewish war profiteers associated with the Social Democratic Party during the Weimar Republic. They were arrested in 1924 and sentenced in 1928 to eleven months' imprisonment.
31 Alexandre Stavisky (1886–1934) was a Jewish French embezzler whose financial crimes involved members of Camille Chautemps' Socialist government. He committed suicide in 1934 but suspicions that the government had murdered him in a cover-up led to Chautemps' resignation.

Europe Explodes

The referendum election between Van Zeeland and Degrelle of 11 April 1937 would offer him the turning point, installed silently he knocked me out in the passage way. At the very last minute of the electoral campaign, when every response was technically impossible, he suddenly waved his staff from the Middle Ages in the air.

With a brutality and especially with an intolerance that, of course, no Catholic public would allow today, he threw himself, mitre on his head, into a strictly electoral quarrel with which Catholicism did not strictly have anything to do, throwing out *urbi et orbi* a fulminating declaration prohibiting people to vote for me based on conscience!

That was not all. He prohibited people besides, and still considering conscience, that is to say, under penalty of sin, from abstaining from voting, which very many Belgian Catholics were inclined to do who, not having rallied to Rex, did not wish nevertheless to give their votes to the candidate put forward by the extreme Left and of whom, besides, people began to whisper that he too was involved in a very ugly financial story.

The scandal burst in the very summer of his election. One learnt then that the protegé of the cardinal had not hesitated before to secretly appropriate, with some accomplices, the payments of high functionaries of the Banque Nationale, dead on the lists of the civil state but whom Van Zeeland and his clique maintained in perfect health on the emoluments page of the official bank of the Belgian state!

Van Zeeland and his brigand colleagues called this slush fund 'the pot'. They emptied it without shame every month, robbing the state and robbing, in addition, indirectly, the tax authorities to whom, one imagines, they did not declare these revenue diversions!

The politico-financial habits of the democracies before 1940 were such that one could perfectly become prime minister after having used corpses of functionaries to fill one's pockets at the expense of the state! Hand on his heart, pouting, the Van Zeeland in question offered himself to the sanctimonious voters, in order to represent in their name the Fatherland and Virtue, put in danger by Rexism! One had to listen to the false apostle, sharper than the millions of appliances fabricated by Mr. Gillette, formal, whining, playing the democratic martyr: 'I advance calmly and serenely on a road filled with ambushes!'

Try a little to repeat ten times rapidly this pebbly gibberish: 'I advance calmly and serenely on a road filled with ambushes!' Then he cast his tearful eyes to the heavens of the Pure and the archbishops!

Never mind! This Maccabean bank robber was, indeed, the number one European champion of the fight against 'Fascism' before the Second World War!

And to save him from the electoral defeat that the polls of the Ministry of the Interior allowed one to clearly foresee three days before the final date, a cardinal did not hesitate, some hours before the election, to wave his staff in all directions like the club of a troglodyte.

He obliged, under penalty of sin, hundred thousand Catholics of Brussels to vote for a pickpocket who, that very year, in October 1937, slid into the scandal of his 'pot', had to leave — forever! — the presidency of the Belgian government, while several of his necrophiliac colleagues of the Banque Nationale — a state minister at their head — committed suicide, within some days, a veritable string of sausages stuffed with dynamite bursting in the air from Brussels to Antwerp!

But on 11 April 1937, the 'pot-man' Van Zeeland, dripping with benedictions, had risen as victor to the altar of anti-Nazism. It is clear that the fact of being Catholic was, in my political life, a considerable handicap. If I had been a non-believer, I would not have been subjected to these abominable pressures, to this blackmail of the consciences of a high clergy which wielded the staff like a club. Or I would have sent the above-mentioned political prelate spinning into the air with his mitre, his 'mules',[32] and his golden staff!

---

32 A prelate's shoes (from the Latin *mulleus calceus*, red shoes).

Europe Explodes

I would have been less bundled, less stuffed with complexes, less isolated because the Catholicism of that time was narrow, vindictive, restricted, and even often, provocative. It raised barriers in all directions. It had deformed us. It cut off millions of honest people from us. And it exposed us to unheard of violences, like those of that maniac with the staff and acorns, banging on the crowd, who thought he had a divine right and was an omnipotent master of everything, including the liberty of the voters.

'The cross has defeated the swastika' proclaimed the Paris *Intransigeant*, on the morrow of the election of Van Zeeland, across the entire breadth of its first page! Such a title of a Freemasonic newspaper said a lot about it! It corresponded to the 'Long live the cardinal, in the name of God!' of the Belgian Marxists hurled in Brussels on the eve of their victory! Léon Blum invited the victor to Paris. He was received like the Belgian Bayard[33] pushed forward against Hitler.

Now — and that was also funny but one learnt it only later — the chief backer of this episcopal anti-Hitlerian had been — for exactly the same sum: six million francs — and at the very same time — the backer of the Hitlerian organisations in Germany.

It was the soda magnate Solvay who, as a perfect hypercapitalist, financed what he thought were two rival clans, in order to have control over both, and get off the hook in any eventuality!

It is under these duplicitous millions and under these barrels of holy water laced with bile, under this deployment of the calumny of 'To Berlin!' repeated endlessly by the war-mongers from London to Paris, that I experienced, during this Van Zeeland eferendum, and though I had obtained 40% more votes than in the previous year, my first electoral failure. I knocked the same Van Zeeland down six months later after having revealed to the Belgian public in all its details the scandal of the famous 'pot'. But the damage was done, the calumny, 'To Berlin!' had crippled me, cutting down my speed.

---

33 Bayard is the bay-coloured magical horse belonging to Reynaud in the mediaeval *chansons de geste*. The Bayard legend is celebrated in many towns in Belgium.

Sensing how this slogan struck the public, the horde of Belgian Marxists thrown against my legs hastened to cover Belgium with notices where I appeared dressed in a spiked helmet as the Germans bore in 1914 at a time when I was only a boy!

From election to election, this spiked helmet would increasingly cover the walls of Belgium, install itself on my head in hundreds of thousands of copies. The Marxist press did not hesitate before anything, not even having recourse to the greatest lies. It published falsified photos where the leader of my members of parliament appeared on the great official stairway of the Nazi rallies of Nuremberg, between two hedges of flags with swastikas!

We found in the agency archives of the original photo where Hitler was to be found instead of our member of parliament! Then the photo of the latter that one had superimposed on the former and which had been taken in front of the parliament in Brussels!

But it was really no use any more getting angry or even protesting. The tribunals turned a deaf ear or buried the documents. Nothing more existed than the hatred of Germany! The avant-garde of the Germans, at that time quite close, where Belgium would be devoured by them, with our complicity!

After the Second World War had ended, all the archives of the Third Reich were seized, dissected. Nowhere did one find the least trace of any place or even of any contact of Rex or of me, before the German invasion of 10 May 1940, with anything connected with the diplomacy of the Third Reich or the propaganda of the Third Reich.

Since 1937, we had watched our step, taking care — and that was lamentable, for useful contacts in all countries could have been useful more than ever — never to meet anywhere an Italian or a German. It was no use.

Instead of advancing electorally, we had to retreat, even while realising with an increasing anxiety that Belgium was, like Europe, henceforth seized with the anti-Hitlerian madness and that, in a time that called for prudence, reserve, it rushed, head bowed, towards the precipice.

One could still believe in 1939, when Poland had been invaded and when the Anglo-French had declared war on the Reich, that Belgium, declaring itself officially neutral, would conserve certain opportunities of remaining outside the conflict.

But these opportunities were squandered a few weeks later. At the beginning of November 1939 an agreement had been concluded between the leader of the French army, General Gamelin, and the Belgian military attaché in Paris, General Delvoie, a secret agreement, as one may imagine !

A French lieutenant colonel named Hautecoeur had immediately been dispatched on a secret mission to Belgium, to the highest authorities, as a faithful retainer of the Allied military chiefs. Gamelin had always been a resolute partisan of the entry of the French army into Belgium, 'the only way' he wrote to Prime Minister Daladier on 1 September 1939, in view of an offensive action which, he added, 'would divert the war from the French frontiers, particularly from our rich eastern frontiers'.

'It was,' Gamelin later explained, in order to justify himself (*Servir*, t.III, p. 243), 'of the highest interest to seek to bring together to the Allied plans the twenty Belgian divisions whose equivalent could not be obtained on our own territory on account of our growing drop in the birthrate.'

'Of course,' he continued, 'I made President Daladier and the British authorities aware through these official and secret conversations.'

'The Belgians', he wrote in conclusion, 'have always made known to me their consent to my proposals'. (*Servir*, t.I, p.89)

On the part of Generalissimo Gamelin the manœuvre was legitimate. He was the leader of the Allied coalition and sought to win the war as surely as possible and with the least cost. He had acted in conformity with his imperatives. 'On 20 September, we had decided to enter into relations with the Belgian government' (*Servir*, t. I, pp. 83 et 84). 'We' was Daladier,[34] the English minister

---

34 Édouard Daladier (1884–1970) was a French Radical Socialist politician who served as Prime Minister of France from 1933 to 1934 and from 1938 to 1940.

of production, Lord Hankey,[35] and the minister of war, Hore Belisha,[36] a Jew as it happened.

This decision had been effective. 'At the beginning of November', Gamelin adds, very naive in his revelations, 'we had arrived at an agreement with the Belgian general staff' (*Servir*, t.I p.84). Nothing would have been risked by denying these scarcely diplomatic affirmations. 'General Gamelin negotiating secretly with the Belgians', Churchill specified (*The Gathering Storm*, p.89) — Pierlot recognised, quite bluntly, but eight years later, in the newspaper *Le Soir* of 9 July 1947: 'When appointed, he was provided with Belgian liaison officers to lend their support to the Franco-British as soon as they entered Belgian territory', adding 'when the Allied armies entered Belgium it was following the dispostions ordered in advance and with mutual accord.'

In politics almost everything is valuable. But still, one should not have at that time acted officially as champions of neutrality, as the Belgian government did with so much fanfare and hypocrisy! And especially, the latter should have taken care to see that the manœuvres now tortuous were not discovered! One can also, in politics, allow oneself the luxury of being cunning, on condition, however, of not getting caught! Now, from the beginning of November 1939, Hitler had been exactly informed of everything. 'Our secrets', Gamelin melancholically realised, 'were permeable on many sides to the espionage of the Germans' (*Servir*, t.I, pp.96 et 97)

This was the case, particularly with regard to its agreement to a secret collaboration with the Belgian government. From 23 November 1939 Hitler informed his generals, army commanders, of it during a meeting at the Chancellery. 'Belgian neutrality in fact does not exist. I have the proof that they have a secret agreement with the French' (Document 789 P.S. of the Nuremberg archives). He even had double proof. 'I knew it from two different sides

---

35 Maurice, Baron Hankey (1877–1963) was Secretary of Lloyd George's War Cabinet during the First World War and also a member of Neville Chamberlain's War Cabinet in 1939.
36 Leslie Hore-Belisha (1893–1957) was a Jewish British politician who served as Secretary of State for War from 1937–1940 under Neville Chamberlain.

in the same week', Hitler told me during the war, one evening, confidentially. He had received two complete reports of the decisions taken by Generalissimo Gamelin, the first provided by an informer of the Allied General Headquarters, the other by a confidant that Hitler had within the French government itself!

Hitler would no doubt have invaded Belgium in any case. A small country was not going to divert his grand war machine at the decisive hour of the march forward. But if he had had scruples still he could, from November 1939, free himself of them without too much remorse since the Belgian neutrality had only been a lie and a trick.

We Rexists, not knowing anything of these underground schemes, not so brilliant as to tell the truth, we continued to lead, as a sacrificed troop, the national combat for a neutrality which remained, in our eyes, one of the final possibilities of saving the peace, and not a negligible possibility even at that time — as the failures of the government of Reynaud proved, who, in a total 'phoney war', saved himself from justice only through a close vote ('and further it was false' President Herriot remarked later). Laval, his almost certain replacement, was inclined to negotiate.

In the evening I sometimes went to see King Léopold III in his palace at Laeken. General Jacques de Dixmude guided me. The sovereign received me in a relaxed fashion, in riding breeches. We fixed the bases of the Rexist press campaign together tending to maintain the Belgian public opinion in an exemplary neutrality.

I hardly suspected in any case that the secret representative in Belgium of the French High Command sat in the same armchair, on other evenings, brought in tip toe like me! What would the Belgians have said if, instead of this agent of Gamelin, a colonel of the Wehrmacht as a secret delegate of Hitler close to the government of so-called neutrality, had come to visit? The double dealing was patent.

Double dealing or, more precisely, triple dealing, for, in March 1940, realising that the affair smelt fishy, King Léopold III, undertaking a new secret about-turn, had sent to Berlin to the minister Goebbels his confidant, the ex-Socialist minister, de Man. The latter recounted to me himself in August 1940 how his mission to the Nazi minister consisted in making known to the Germans the interest that there would be for them to slip into the southern side of Belgium and drive into Sedan, the Somme and Abbeville. Hitler had thought of it a little before him! But that explains some things. And notably why it would have been difficult for Léopold III to dash off to London on 28 May 1940, certain of hearing, some hours later Goebbels unwrap the package before the microphones! In short, everything was hopeless! The dice had been cast.

Through provocations and deliberate misunderstanding the warmongers of the west had arrived at their goal, to make a Hitler at the end of his tether come out of his den. When it is a matter of the Soviets in 1954 (Budapest) and in 1968 (Prague), one had other arrangements!

The 'useless and stupid' war (as Spaak[37] said) was thus going to start.

On 10 May 1940, the powerful caterpillar tracks of Hitler's tanks broke down the gates of the west, crushing under them, for more than thousand kilometres, discredited, crazy, irremediably outdated democratic governments.

---

37 Paul-Henri Spaak (1899–1972) was a Belgian Socialist politician who served as Foreign Minister under van Zeeland in 1936. He was Prime Minister of Belgium between 1938 and 1939 and, from 1940, served as Foreign Minister in the Belgian government in exile in London. At the outbreak of the war he advocated Belgian neutrality with regard to the developments in Germany and France. He was Prime Minister of Belgium again between 1946 and 1949, and was also instrumental in the preparation of the 1957 Treaty of Rome which established the European Economic Community.

Chapter V
Hitler, for a Thousand Years

Never did people know a suprise, a panic, an 'everyman for himself' as desperate as the French, the Belgians, the Dutch, the Luxemburgers did when the armies of the Third Reich invaded them on the 10 May 1940. However, normally, all must have known what to expect. Already in September 1939 the debacle of the Polish had been significant. 'In five days our cavalry will be in Berlin', the latter had proclaimed, with a Dali moustache, a carbuncle eye, one week before the first act of the conflict.

The Polish would have been able to improvise, calm their warmongers a little, take Hitler at his word and begin negotiations, even if it were only to equivocate, that he had proposed to them two days before the event. The slushes of the Polish autumns were approaching: the tidal wave that was going to submerge their country in three weeks would, at least, have been delayed. In diplomacy time is sovereign. A good diplomat is one who has his briefcase full of excuses for delay.

Poland was complacent enough to defy, up to the catastrophe, a Hitler whose accomplice they had been on the day in the very recent past when it had, at Teschen, carved for itself a good beefsteak in the plunder of Czechoslovakia.

But the English, who saw their pawns eclipsing everywhere in the Balkans, had immediately shaken up the Polish with foolish promises, instead of showing disgust to them for their participation in the carving up of the Czech territories. The British interest had largely carried them over moral concerns. But in September 1939, when the Polish, brought to a boiling point by London, found itself invaded, the English did not appear either at Danzig or at Warsaw and Poland fell into a frightful loss.

This loss the whole world had witnessed. But the reactions of the Allied general staffs had been strictly nil. Generalissimo Gamelin, as soon as he had to keep his commitments from 1 September 1939, hurried to announce solemnly that he would intervene, but adding that he would need twenty three full days to have the stew of a French backup-offensive simmer in the casseroles of his offices.

As for the English, some weeks passed before they disembarked on the quays of Calais the first packages of white cigarettes of their intervention troops . . . in France. 'We will dry our linen on the Siegfried line', they shouted when the said English linen was still waiting, in the London depots, to be freed of its mothballs! In any case, neither then nor ever would a British combatant appear at the Vistula.

It was the Soviets and not the English who, six years later, moved the Germans out of Poland and claim it for themselves!

In the meanwhile, corporal Hitler had dominated the pretentious military chiefs of the west, including those of his own country. All these brilliant specialists, tasselled, medalled, covered in ringing tinware, had thought that it would be sufficieint for them, as always, to draw out of drawers thick files where everything, dating far back, had been meticulously foreseen. The 'Bohemian' corporal had cast aside, without any ado, these redtapes.

His conservative strategists only envisaged, in 1939, partial operations in the north of the Polish territory. They knew everything of course. But the corporal, corporal that he was, had thought out, in his brain, in all details, the tactic of the Blitzkrieg, an artillery of breaching tank divisions coupled with air artilleries.

Hardly had the Poles had the time to refill their fountain pens, which would allow them, on their entry into Berlin, to send victorious post-cards to their wonder-struck girlfriends, than the Stukas, violently opening the path to several thousands of grouped tanks, tumbled down from the sky on all the vital points and cut them into slivers like an American beefsteak.

From the first day of the war, every contact with the interior of the Polish territory was dead, or condemned to death. From the first week, under the protective roof of aircrafts, the enormous pincers of the troops fortified by Hitler closed their shears on all sides in the east, forming fishtraps at the depths of which the million Polish fish that were taken in the bait writhed desperately, their belly scales already dry.

At the end of the month of September 1939, Colonel Beck, who should have, at that time, been having his horse drink in the Spree or emptying the cellars of Horcher, fled to Romania, leaving his people high and dry, entirely invaded and annihilated.

It was a complete revolution of the methods of war that had been accomplished, under the nose of the hundreds of millions of spectators of the two worlds. But wait! Why should one have allowed oneself to be impressed? A general is a general and he knows everything! A corporal is a corporal and he does not know anything! Militarily, all the facts foreseen for centuries by specialists of general staffs had been destroyed. However, they had nothing to learn from anybody, especially from a low Bohemian subaltern at that!

It was in this way that, 10 May 1940 found Generalissimo Gamelin caressing the feathers of his carrier-pigeons in his headquarters in Vincennes, with outdated and useless telephones, whereas in a wonderful coupling of land and air forces, all of a terrifying efficiency and promptitude, the armies of the ignorant coporal, applying for a second time a revolutionary strategy that the experts of the military bureaucracy of the continent had rejected with a stinging contempt, repeated the blow of the invasion of Poland.

They would in eleven days cut into two from Sedan to Dunkirk, a continent that four years of classic assault, from August 1914 to July 1918, had not been able to tear apart, even by sacrificing several million dead men.

Hundred thousand young Germans — the only ones who, in fact, were in touch during the campaign of France of 1940 — applying the strategic plans of the chief corporal, cordoned off two thousand French generals, still farting on the previous evening with self-importance, and two million of their soldiers discomfited, tattered, whom a new science of war had just squashed.

There was not only, for warning people, the Polish invasion of September 1939, there had been also the Norwegian invasion of April 1940, there too everything had been new. One had seen, in the Chancellery in Berlin, corporal Hitler holding for eight hours, in front of an immense mural map of Scandinavia, the attention of all the chiefs of the forces, commanders of battalions included, who were going to have to play a role in the disembarkment — of an audacity without precedent — that Hitler had prepared in the most rigorously absolute secrecy.

Imagine that! Whereas in the past, one, or three or four massive and monocled generals of choice received for execution orders typed in twelve copies, a war leader without golden epaulettes explained by himself to each officer concerned in the action the exact role that he would have to fulfil, indicated it to him on the map, made him repeat aloud the orders as well as the presentation of the precise manœuvre that he would have to effect.

The audacity! A solid buffet had been set up in the hall where each one, without ceremony, pinched as he pleased a sandwich when he was hungry and ate it with full mouth two steps from the Führer!

Hitler himself had been, before, secretly sailed by ship all along the coast to be invaded. He knew each cove of the disembarkment. Agent 007 would not have done better ! The young officer who left the Chancellery left dazed at having been received with such simplicity by the supreme leader of his army.

He was fired up. He had seen that the affair had been prepared with care by a connaisseur, doubling as an expert. In a few days, the operation was secured whereas, however, the expeditionary Franco-English corps, set in motion before that of Hitler, was mired down in its *impedimenta*, and had its feet frozen in the snows and its head broken by the bombs of Stukas. All the glorious plans and prognostics of the superspecialists of the western general staffs had evaporated. The generals of Gamelin, seven months after the fall of Warsaw, had been ridiculed a second time, stuffed under the clutter of their science, monumental and dead, like the pyramids.

No matter! They continued to talk ironically in the halls of Vincennes about this grotesque corporal who claimed to know more than the professionals of military science, theoretical and applied! The said professionals, at the end of a month of campaign in France, met, like General Giraud,[38] exhausted, open-necked, in the field of a prisoner camp, or else, had fled crawling for thousand kilometres, soaked, out of breath, undid their belt and got their breath painfully in the last castles of the last buttresses of the Pyrenees range.

Millions of deserters, crazed, had done in a week what the Tour de France does with much more difficulty in a month. Haggard, exhausted, they had left the detours of their desertion filled with bags, astrakhan coats and grandmothers dead of exhaustion, whose abandoned corpses rotted in the sun among the blackened quarters of horses and cows.

They had been the living image — or, more precisely, agonising — of an old ossified world, that a new world, new bodies and new minds overwhelmed. It was not a defeat, it was a burial, the burial of the Europe of dad, it was the emergence of a generation that considered the universe with the eyes of those at the beginning of creation.

The young Germans could one day be crushed in their turn — and they were. But they had created something irreparable, destroyed an epoch, beautiful perhaps for the wealthy like Boni de Castellane[39] or the pederasts like Proust, sinister for others, a corpse-like epoch that thousands of meat flies already surrounded with their whirls when the old Marshal Pétain, chewing his moustaches, raised his white flag, in the supreme week of adventure, at the end of June 1940.

---

38 General Henri Giraud (1879–1949) was a French general who was captured in both World Wars. He escaped both times, the second time in 1942.
39 Boni de Castellane (1867–1932) was a French marquis who was a fashionable socialite of the Belle Époque.

Hitler, for the first time in his life, had raised his eyes towards the cupola of the Paris Opera and looked down towards the porphyry tomb of Napoleon, a pink motionless boat in a bowl of grey marble. The swastika unfurled its long scarlet trail from the Arctic Ocean to Bidasoa.[40] The entire west had been knocked unconscious, dazed, not having yet understood anything except that everything was lost, that the rusty machinery of the old countries — the parties, governments, newspapers — lay in the ditches like scrap iron of the war material battered and burnt by the *Panzers*. It seemed to everybody that no country would ever reemerge from such an abyss.

Only an unknown de Gaulle leaned from his London balcony towards the old lady France who had collapsed skirt in the air, chignon crushed, at the bottom of the black hole of the hexagon. Apart from the wishful thinking of this fireman without an escape-ladder, there was no Frenchman, Belgian or Luxemburger or Dutchman left who believed in the resurrection of the democratic world reduced to ashes in some weeks.

'One thought Germany was the master of Europe for thousand years', repeated the Belgian minister Spaak — crimson, bald head gleaming, his clothes drenched — who sadly carried round, in July 1940, his spongy rotundities from inn to inn in the Auvergne valleys.

Everybody in his way had lived through an adventure. One of the least funny had been ours, Belgian Rexists. For, in France as well as in Brussels, the mainstream press had repeated to satiety that we were Hitlerians, the French police had pounced on us in the first hour of hostilities. It had grabbed twelve thousand of us and had marched us to its jails and its concentration camps.

We had been dragged from prison to prison, treated with a barbaric fury in torture chambers, thrashed hundred times, jaws demolished by blows of bunches of keys, our mouths kept open so that our jailiers could pour their urine into them. I speak of what I experienced personally. I had been condemned to death in Lille,

---

40 The Bidasoa is a river that runs between the Basque Country of northern Spain and southern France.

already in the first week. My twenty one comrades in suffering in our prison truck were all murdered like dogs near the music kiosk of Abbeville on 20 May 1940. None of their executioners — of the French military men, alas! — knew even their names. Among them there were women: a young girl, her mother, her grandmother. The latter had, before dying, her breast punctured thirty times with a bayonet!

A young priest who, during the last two days, had held against his cheekbone an eye that a sadistic guard had gouged out of its socket was butchered like the others with a furious blow of the fist.

Not one of all of us prisoners escaped this frightful massacre apart from me alone because my executioners imagined that by forcing me to become a martyr — ten teeth broken in a single night — I would reveal to them Hitler's offensive plans, of which I knew nothing, as you may imagine! My temporary survival was thus important to the Intelligence Services.

The rapidity of the military development caused it to be transformed into a prolonged survival which I still benefit from today. But finally, emerging from the French prison camp, I found myself helpless like the others. What was going to happen? The old political, social, economic system of the west had been thrown to the ground like a deck of cards trampled on and useless forever. And then what?

The armies of the Reich were stationed everywhere. The German system was installed everywhere. The France of Vichy of summer 1940 was only a poor congress of emasculated ex-politicians and ignorant generals, seated at tables in mediocre hotel halls of a watering town that was truly symbolic, for France had sunk. In the north, the Dutch had seen their queen rolling up her numerous skirts fly post-haste to London, and then to Canada.

The grand-duchess of Luxembourg, who had come from a system of female primary school teachers of the 19th century, had also left for the prim British countryside. Between these two countries, the King of the Belgians, Léopold III, a neurasthenic whose worn out nerves paid the cost of an ancestral syphilis, was confined in his castle in the Brussels suburbs. The only former minister who had remained by his side, Henri de Man, the president of the Belgian Socialist Party just the previous evening, had rallied in a showy way to Hitler, without any result besides.

Since in 1940 only the rivers had remained in place, de Man was content to go fishing, nothing political. The framework of the states, the social status, the economy, even the most elementary possibilities of earning one's living, had been overturned. One had seen even those convicted under common law, their hair short under their cap, their feet naked in large clogs, on the sides of the main roads plundering groceries, in good spirits, besides. Hundreds of ambulances, hospitals, packed with fleeing civilians, had ended up with their mattresses and canaries, in the courtyards of the schools of Languedoc or Roussillon. There were no more policemen, no more firefighters, no more undertakers between the Frise and the Marne. They wiped their brows on the benches of the public gardens of Nîmes or Carcassonne. Millions of dislocated refugees turned up from all sides.

And, above all, the troubling question returned: what is going to become of our countries? what is Hitler thinking of, what does he want? Is he going to annex us? Is he going to impose Gauleiters on us?

In fact, the people would have accepted anything, provided that one returned their livelihood to them, their Pernod, their beds and their slippers. But for those who had made the salvation of their fatherland the only reason of their existence the question of the survival of their country, of their future destiny, was planted like a sting in their heart and tore at it at every sigh.

The fate of every occupied country in 1940, whether it was big and rich like France, or miniscule like the Grand Duchy of Luxembourg with its three towns and its four shale rocks, was in the hands of Hitler and nobody else.

What remained of free territory in France could be conquered in forty eight hours. Marshal Pétain, trotting around in his room in a hotel provided with a lift, had less power guaranteed him than a metro driver or a gate-keeper gulping down his calvados.⁴¹

As for Belgium, would it reappear one day? Would it be attached to the Reich, more or less openly? In two or three different, rival sections? Germans of Eupen and of Malmédy? The Flemish, encouraged by the occupier, who would shake themselves feverishly into a narrow nationalism? Walloons who no longer even knew what they were, nor what they would become: former Belgians? future Frenchmen? second-class Germans? A colonised territory that the Flemish nationalists would obtain as a Lebensraum?

When I returned to Brussels, coming out finally from my French prisons, bearded, emaciated, shattered, I felt, in spite of everything that was at that time thinkable, seized with a profound despair.

For the general public, assailed during the last two years of the pre-war years by waves of lies, I was Hitler's man. Now, I did not know the first thing about what that could mean in relation to my country. I did not even know where to camp. My own property in the forest of Soignes was occupied by the Germans.

I was their so-called man. Now my house had been invaded by them without any explanation. Fifty pilots camped there. Going up surprised to my room I had found, quite naked and on my bed, an enormous colonel of the Luftwaffe, crimson like a gigantic lobster fabricated for a science-fiction film. I had no other way, during the first days, than to sleep on a camp bed at the home of one of my sisters.

I have said it hundred times: we had nothing to do with the Germans. And this huge military man installed on my bed, his skin shining with sweat, said enough of the instability of my fate and of the non-existence of any plans that the great Reich could have fabricated around me.

We were nationalists, but Belgian nationalists. And Belgium had, at that time, sunk like a stone. Its future was completely blocked, obscure like a tunnel of which one did not know if the final exit was walled, and if it would become again one day more or less usable.

---

41 Fruit brandy from Normandy.

Such was my drama as the chief nationalist returning to my own country occupied by the forces of a foreign statesman, to whom I was said to be closely connected and of whom I did not for a long time know what sort of political edification and what basis of agreement he imagined for each of our countries within the Europe that his iron fist forged. What survival would he allow my people? It was a total mystery.

Chapter VI
Alongside the Germans

The months of the end of 1940 and the beginning of 1941 were not funny for anybody in Europe, not more in Belgium than elsewhere. Nobody spoke of the Dutch. They were no doubt going to be included in the geographical complex of Greater Germany. The Grand Duchy of Luxembourg equally, from all the evidence.

As for the French they had already begun fighting amongst themselves under the contemptuous eye of the occupiers, with a stubbornness that would clearly have been more effective behind an anti-tank cannon in June 1940. A month after having established the bases of the collaboration with Hitler, Marshal Pétain had thrown overboard his prime minister Pierre Laval, whom the Germans did not like, whose dirty nails, yellow teeth, and crow skin displeased Hitler but whose cleverness, good nature, 'Auvergne' sense of horse-trading and adaptation ambassador Abetz, at that time very much apparent at Berchtesgaden, appreciated. Laval, sarcastic, agitating his cigarettes under his burnt moustaches, had replied tit for tat and treated the Marshal like an old disaffected trooper's uniform.

In short, it was total confusion. It would last until the last day, in France, and even outside France, at the castle of exile of Sigmaringen,[42] where the French 'collaborators' fled, into the sombre corridors of the reconstructed feudal fortress, peopled with huge and sinister armour.

---

[42] Sigmaringen is a town in Baden-Württemberg noted for its castle of the Hohenzollerns. In September 1944, following the Allied invasion of France, Philippe Pétain and members of the Vichy government set up a government in exile there.

There remained our case, the Belgians, the most complicated case. I had been able to give up contacts with the King Léopold, prisoner, chained by Hitler and unchained by the family nurse, whom he married, promoted suddenly to Princess of Rethy. His secretary, Baron Capelle, served as a courier to us. He had advised me energetically on behalf of the sovereign — and I had taken great care to note down his words immediately — to make an effort to build a bridge with the victor.

Ambassador Abetz, a colourful friend with whom I had spent, in 1936, a week's vaction in South Germany and whose wife had been raised, at the same time as mine, in a French boarding school of Sacré-Cœur, was a very curious person. He liked non-conformists especially. After my odyssey as a prisoner, he had invited me, several times, to have breakfast or dinner with him in his embassy in Paris, in the ravishing palace of Queen Hortense, on rue de Lille.

He set up an entire fanfare of the Wehrmacht in the garden, below our small table, for the pleasure of making the left bank of the Seine resound with loud musical sounds. We had studied together all the future possibilities of Beligum. He had gone to Berchtesgaden to speak of this problem with the Führer. He had recalled to him our interview of 1936, and had repeated to him the impression that it had made on him at that time. He persuaded Hitler to invite me. He saw to it that a car would come shortly to pick me up in Brussels, asking me to hold myself ready to leave for Berchtesgaden at any time.

I waited.

I would wait three years before finally meeting Hitler, under the sombre pine trees of the Lithuanian forest, one night when, wounded three or four times during seventeen hand-to-hand combats, having broken, on the previous evening, the encirclement of Cherkasy in Ukraine, I had been taken in the personal plane of Hitler, in order that he might hang around my neck the chain of the Ritterkreuz. But three years had been lost.

Everything failed in October 1940, I learnt later, because the Flemish leaders, at the instigation of the German Security services who dreamed of breaking Belgium into two, had made known that an accord between Hitler and a Walloon would meet with the opposition of the Flemish party of Belgium.

This was stupid and absolutely contrary to the truth. I had, in 1936, obtained at the elections almost as many votes in Flanders as in Wallonia. And an accord with the chief Flemish nationalists themselves had, in 1937, coordinated our political conceptions and our plan of action.

But, since some German espionage services stated that an arrangement with me would end in unleashing very violent linguistic oppositions in a combat zone, the chief base of the aerial battle of Germany against England, Hitler put off the negotiations until later. That was an impasse, absolute darkness.

After the cancellation of my interview, King Léopold himself tried, against all odds, to meet Hitler. His sister, the hereditary princess of Italy, wife of Humberto, at that time priviliged ally of the Reich, a powerfully built young woman, long legs, clear and hard eyes, had gone to Berchtesgaden to contact the Führer again, with the stubbornness that women are able to deploy, sometimes at the wrong time.

Hitler had finally received Léopold III, but coldly. He had not revealed anything to him. The interview was limited to that distribution of warm drinks, less revealing even than coffee grounds. The mistake had been complete.

Everything that we did during the winter of 1940–1941 to melt the German iceberg washed up again on our shores, and did not lead us very far. Our advances — notably during a big meeting that I gave at the Palais des Sports after the New Year — did not have any other result than some lines of banal reportage in the *Völkischer Beobachter*.

Deep down did Hitler himself know at that time what he wanted? As General de Gaulle said in May 1968, when the revolution of the students of the Sorbonne almost sank him, 'the situation was difficult to seize'. Was the war against the English going to be prolonged? Or, as General Weygand believed and said, was the

United Kingdom going to fall to its knees, suddenly, crushed under the iron and fire?

And the Soviets? Molotov, a busybody under his spectacles, had come in October 1940, to bring to Hitler — besides the spectacle of his odd appearance as a business traveller with trousers waving like a tyre — the list of copious dishes that Stalin wanted to be offered shortly.

The armies of the Third Reich had hardly swept half of Europe than the Soviets wanted to allocate to themselves, without expense and without risks, the other half of the continent! Already, profiting from the Polish campaign in 1939, Stalin had swallowed the three Baltic states with the vigorous bite of an inatiable glutton. He had repeated it, in June 1940, devouring Bessarabia. Now, what he demanded was nothing more or less than the complete control of the Balkans.

Hitler had been the enemy number one of the Soviets. Very reluctantly, in order not be led into having to combat on two fronts from the beginning of the war, he had marked a stop, in August 1939, in his fight against Communism. But it was impossible that he would permit the installation of the Soviets at the very border of the continent that he had just collected together.

The threat was clear. The danger was not only great but it was evident. Hitler could not let himself be surprised by an incursion of the Russians on the Reich if a great reverse in the west would strike him one day. He had to be ready to forestall a bad stroke about the possibilities of which the threats emerging from the small mouth of the yellow weasel of a Molotov hardly left any doubt.

Initiating the action, Hitler had secretly started the preparations for the Operation Barbarossa, the elaboration of the plans of which had been confided to General Paulus, who would be vanquished at Stalingrad.

In the meanwhile, everything in Europe remained indecisive. The internal divisions of the French and the rapid dissolution of a politics of rapprochement with Pétain had counselled Hitler to let time pass and the affairs of the west subside. The morale of the different peoples of the east wilted. Oppositions of race, language, clans, ambitions eroded them without any big action or at least a great hope raising them.

For me it was clear : two years, three years, of such a stagnation and Belgium would be ripe for dissolution, absorption, more or less direct, by the Flemish into a unified Germany, and the discarding of the Walloons neutralised, emasculated Europeans, neither French nor German; and the silent elimination of a King Léopold, who had become totally invisible, separated from his people, moving between his empty library and a nursery that was less isolated but which, nevertheless, politically did not lead very far.

Hope to see Hitler again? There was no longer even a question of a meeting. Discuss with the underlings in Brussels? They had no power of discussion. They were, besides, gorged with the self-importance of victorious military men treating defeated civilians from a height. We detested each another with equal vigour. One should be able one day to discuss with Hitler as equals and with the victorious Reich. But how? The political horizon remained desperately impenetrable.

It was then that, suddenly on 22 June 1941, the preventive war against the Soviets broke out, accompanied by Hitler's call for volunteers from all of Europe for a combat that would no longer be the combat of the Germans alone but of Europeans in solidarity. For the first time since 1940 a *European* plan appeared.

Run to the Eastern Front?

Clearly it would not be the modest Belgian contingents that we would be able to assemble in the beginning that would cause Stalin to hit the dust! Among millions of combatants we would be only a handful.

But courage could compensate for the small numbers. Nothing would prevent us from fighting like lions, from acting with an exceptional valour, to make the enemy of yesterday to confirm that their combat comrades of today were strong, that their nation had not proven unworthy, that they could, one day, in the new Europe, be a vigorous element worthy of action.

And then, there was no other solution. Certainly the Allies could also win.

But frankly how many Europeans who had been invaded believed in the autumn of 1940 and at the beginning of 1941 in this victory of the Allies? ten percent? five percent? Were these five percent more lucid than we? Who would prove it?

The Americans, without whom a collapse of the Third Reich was not even imaginable in 1941, still held to a policy of running with the hare and hunting with the hounds. Their opinion remained, for the most part, clearly isolationist. All the polls and the public opinion in the United States established that and repeated it at every new poll.

As for the Soviets, who would have imagined in 1941 that their resistance would be as tenacious as it was? Churchill himself declared to his close friends that the destruction of Russia by Germany would be a matter of a few weeks.

The probable thing, for a European in 1941, was thus that Hitler would win, that he would become truly 'the master of Europe for a thousand years' that Spaak had announced to us. In this case, it was not by wallowing in the troubled and sterile swamp of indecisiveness, in Brussels, Paris and Vichy, that titles could be acquired assuring the defeated of 1940 a proportionate participation in history, in the virtues and possibilities of their fatherlands in tomorrow's Europe.

That having been understood it was a matter of giving an example. I was not however going to encourage my followers to rush to the front line between Murmansk and Odessa without being one of them, without sharing with them the sufferings and dangers of combats!

I therefore enlisted, though I was a father of five children. And I enlisted as a simple soldier, in order that the most disadvantaged of our comrades might see me sharing with him his pains and his misfortunes. I had not even advised the Germans of my decision. Two days after I had made it public, a telegram from Hitler announced to me that he had named me an officer. I refused immediately. I went to Russia to acquire the rights that would permit me to discuss honourably one day the conditions of the survival of my country, and not to receive stripes before the first gunshot that would only be operetta stripes.

I became (during four harassing years of combat) corporal, then sergeant, then officer, then senior officer, but every time it was 'for an act of valour in combat', after having, in the course of seventy five hand-to-hand combats, previously drenched my epaulettes in the blood of seven wounds.

'I shall see Hitler', I declared to my close friends at the moment of departure, 'only when he will tie around my neck the ribbon of the Ritterkreuz.'

Thus, precisely, did things transpire three years later. At that moment I could speak clearly, wounded several times, decorated several times, having effected a rupture of the Soviet front that had blown up eleven encircling divisions. And I was going to obtain from Hitler — the written proof of it still exists — a statute recognising for my country, within the heart of the new Europe, a space and possibilities superior to everything that it had known, even at the most glorious times of its history under the dukes of Burgundy and under Charles Quint.

Of the existence of these agreements nobody can doubt any longer. The French ambassador François-Poncet, who hardly likes me, published them in the *Figaro*, with a supporting map.

Hitler was defeated. Thus, our agreement, obtained at the cost of so many sufferings, so much blood and in spite of so many falls, remained without any result. But the contrary could have happened. Eisenhower writes in his *Memoirs* that, even at the beginning of 1945, there remained for Hitler possibilities of winning.

In war, until the last rifle has fallen, everything remains possible. Besides, we did not prevent the Belgians who believed in the London solution from sacrificing themselves in the same way, to assure themselves — in the case of the victory of the other 'bloc' — of the renewal and resurrection of our country. They could not have, any more than we, had an easy life subjected certainly to traps and to intrigues of all sorts. The example of de Gaulle and the sly persecutions of which he was the object from the side of the English and especially the Americans, the humiliations that he had to tolerate, must have been of the same order as the bad luck that we had to suffer many times from the German side before seeing that our cause was assured of success.

In London as in our camp it was necessary to hold steady, not let oneself be intimidated, be, always, one with the interests of one's people. In spite of the risks, it was useful, I was going to say indispensable, that, on both sides, nationalists tried their separate opportunities, in order that our fatherlands would survive, whatever the final chapter of the conflict might be.

This was not a reason, however, why those who found themselves on the side of the victors in 1945 should cut the throats of the others.

Thus very diverse motives animated our minds and our hearts when we left, packs on backs, for the Eastern Front. We went — first objective, official objective — to combat Communism.

But the fight against Communist could have perfectly taken place without us. We left also — the second objective, and in fact the essential objective in our opinion — not exactly to combat the Germans but that we might impose ourselves on the Germans who, intoxicated by their innumerable victories, could have treated us badly in each of our occupied countries.

Some had already shown this, and their prolonged duplicity did not fail to scandalise us many times. After the epic of the Russian Front, it became difficult for them to sabotage again the representatives of peoples who had fought courageously alongside their armies, in a combat which made us all united. That was the great motive of our departure: to force the attention and adherence of the victorious Germans, by edifying with them a Europe that our blood too would have cemented.

We were going to live horrible years in Russia, know physically, morally, a Calvary that cannot be named. In the history of mankind there was never a war that was atrocious to this degree, in endless snows, in endless slush.

Often starving, always without rest, we were overwhelmed with misery, wounds, sufferings of all sorts. To arrive finally at a disaster that engulfed our youth and destroyed our lives . . .

But, what counts in life? Even the apparently useless gift is never that completely. One day it finds its meaning. The huge martyrdom of millions of soldiers, the long gasp of a youth that sacrificed itself totally on the Russian Front, provided in advance to Europe the spiritual compensation indispensable for its renewal.

A Europe of shopkeepers would not have been sufficient. A Europe of heroes was also necessary. The latter would be created before the other, in the course of four years of frightful combats.

Chapter VII
The Tramways of Moscow

Hitler's war in the USSR, begun on 22 June 1941, started well and badly. It started well. The immense machinery of the German army set off with a perfect precision. There were, here and there, some hitches, colonels who got lost, bridges collapsed under the weight of tanks. But these were only details.

From the very first hour the Luftwaffe had, over months, reduced the Soviet airforce to impotence, and rendered the enemy concentrations impossible. At the end of ten days, the Wehrmacht had triumphed everywhere, had spread itself very far everywhere. A total collapse of the Russian Front and of the Soviet regime could come about in a short time. Winston Churchill, more than anybody else, feared these and, in his secret dispatches, warned of them.

However, the war had also started off badly. And it would finish badly precisely becasue it had started badly. First of all — and this was a decisive factor — it had started late, very late, too late, five weeks after the dated fixed by Hitler because the mad adventure of Mussolini at the Greek border, in October 1940, had torpedoed the Hitlerian plans in the east.

It was in the muddy mountains that separate Greece from Albania that the fate of the Second World War was in fact played out, more than at Stalingrad, more than at El Alamein, more than on the beaches of Normandy, more than on the Rhine bridge of Remagen, which was taken intact in March 1945 by the American general Patton. Mussolini was haunted by Hitler's victories. He, the father of Fascism, had been relegated to a secondary role by the series of violent — and always triumphant — campaigns that the

The Tramways of Moscow

Führer had conducted, beating the drum, from Danzig to Lemberg, from Narwik to Rotterdam, from Anvers to Biarritz.

Every time the German eagles had been hoisted on the countries, sometimes enormous, conquered in a trice, while several million prisoners had advanced, like interminable lines of caterpillar tracks, towards the lodging camps of a Reich that was increasingly sure of its successes.

Mussolini, militarily, had spoiled everything. His invasion, *in extremis*, in the French Alps, had ended in a humiliating failure. Marshal Badoglio[43] — a very interested pawn who had collected in his home massive treasures in gold, from Addis Ababa, stolen from the palace of the Negus,[44] who had fled — had, before June 1940, revealed his tactical incapacity, worthy of his follower Gamelin.

While France was on its knees, when the tanks of Guderian and Rommel were deployed almost without combat as far as Provence and a descent to Nice should have been for the Italians only a brief military excursion among yards of fresh fruit, Badoglio, who, however had had at his disposal long months to prepare, had claimed from Mussolini twenty one extra days to shine the nuts and bolts of his soldiers.

The operation had quickly turned into a mess. The French had struck the aggresors hard at the last minute, inflicting on them considerable losses and nailing them to the ground, with their golden brown plumes pathetically dishevelled.

In Africa, the start in Libya had hardly been more brilliant; an Italian general had been made prisoner on the very first day. When the Italian artillery had afforded itself the luxury of hitting a plane that shone in the bright sunlight, it found that it was that of Marshal Balbo. He was brought down like a partridge. In this way, the most famous pilot killed by the Italians in 1940 had been their most glorious leader!

---

43 Marshal Pietro Badoglio (1871–1956) was an Italian general during both World Wars. In early 1943 the king Victor Emmanuel decided secretly to replace Mussolini with Badoglio as prime minister. An armistice was signed on behalf of Badoglio with the Allies in September of that year.
44 The Negus is the monarch of Ethiopia.

Time had not sorted anything out. The Italian arsenal, vaunted flashily for twenty years, was deficient. The navy lacked zeal. The trooper did not feel guided. Marshal Graziani, a muddled mind, a mediocre coach, preferred to give his orders from fifteen metres underground than from fifteen metres in front of his troops as General Rommel, the intrepid Landsknecht,[45] would do later on the Italian Front. Mussolini raged. He was furious about all his failures.

He imagined that he would regild his military shield in the course of an easy conquest of Greece, which would be prepared by millions allotted discreetly to the political personnel at Athens. In this way the victory would be obtained without great conflict, over an enemy that had agreed in advance to cede, and which would resist only in form.

'I had bought everybody up! These Greek bastards pocketed my millions and tricked me!' This surprising confidence was made to me personally by Count Ciano, Italian Minister of External Affairs, of a bright mind and rather rascally on the edges, in June 1942 when, on a whirlwind flight to Rome, I saw him for the last time and asked him about this Greek war, lost in such an extraordinary manner.

Based on these declarations of Ciano (his son-in-law) Mussolini hurried events in October 1940. He did not breathe a word of this invasion plan to Hitler. When the German Chancellor, who was at Hendaye, where he had just met General Franco, got wind of such a plan, he immediately had his special train directed to Italy, where he was welcomed two days later on the quays of Florence by a triumphant Mussolini. 'My troops have just disembarked in Greece this morning!' Hitler had arrived too late! He could only wish his colleague good luck.

But he trembled. And with reason. At the end of some days, the Italian troops who had been devoured in Greece, in the mountain chain of the Pindus, were knocked around, torn apart, pushed back from Epirus in an increasingly tragic debacle.

---

45 A Landsknecht is a German mercenary of Renaissance Europe.

The Italian leaders, boasting on the first day, panic-stricken on the second, had behaved lamentably. The soldiers were annihilated. We saw the moment when the Italian expeditionary corps was about to jump all together into the Adriatic and when the whole of Albania would be overcome by the white skirts of the Greeks. It was necessary, the height of humiliation, to appeal to Hitler, who dispatched German rescue forces in all haste to Tirana.

The situation was restored, but the essential thing was not there alone. That the Greeks had claimed for themselves Albania, a rather vain excrescence of the Italian empire, would not have been specially tragic. King Victor Emmanuel would have borne on his head one crown less. He would have been shortened twenty centimetres during state ceremonies, which would not have been frightening at all.

What was frightening was that the entry of the Greeks into the war had provoked the landing of the English, who had become allies indirectly in Greece. Now, the English installed in the lower Balkans meant the possibility, the near certainty, of seeing them cut the lines of the east when Hitler would thrust himself very deep into the immense Soviet space.

To that was added the fear of the raids of the British airforce, installed in strength in its new Greek bases. It could, under massive bombings, set the Romanian oil-wells afire that were indispensable to the provisions of the twenty Panzer divisions that Hitler prepared to thrust across two thousand kilometres of the Soviet border. The risks had become enormous.

They became absolutely frightful when, in the same winter, the Yugoslavia of King Peter,[46] at the instigation of English agents, confronted the Germans. From that time there was no possible rush, on the planned date, into the USSR, so much less now that Molotov had just sent to the Yugoslav king particularly insolent congratulations from Stalin and the assurance of his moral support.

---

46 Peter II (1923–1970) was the last king of Yugoslavia. Germany attacked Yugoslavia and Greece in April 1941 and Peter was forced to leave the country and set up a government in exile in London.

Following this foolish Mussolinian adventure Hiter, before retaking the east on his grand plan, found himself condemned to clean the Balkans first, to hurtle down all of Yugoslavia with his tanks, all of Greece and even to seize the English aircraft carrier that the island of Crete had become. It was a sensational rush.

In ten days Yugoslavia was conquered and entiredly occupied. Then it was a descent at breakneck speed upto Athens and Sparta. The swastika shone above the gilded marbles of the Acropolis. The parachutists of Goering descended with a triumphant heroism on the island of Crete where the rout of the English was effected in forty eight hours. The Allied ships in flight towards Egypt were sunk like ducks on the Landes ponds.

Perfect. The threat had been removed. But five weeks had been lost, five weeks that Hitler would never again recover.

As a soldier I knew — for we traversed Russia entirely on foot — each detail of this tragedy. It is because Hitler did not have a month that the war did not end in 1941, on the Russian Front, that month that, precisely, the wounded self-esteem of Mussolini had caused the Axis to lose through his lamentable escapade of the Greek border. The time had been lost. And equipment of the highest importance too had been lost.

Not indeed that the German tanks had been destroyed in a great number during the staggered combats of Belgrade on the canal of Corinth. But the heavy equipment of the Panzer Divisions had been seriously jeopardised in the course of three thousand kilometres of trails through mountains and valleys, often very stony.

Hundreds of tanks had to be examined. They could not be utilised on 22 June 1941 during the great start. I say what I saw, saw with my own eyes: the fortified von Kleist divisions, of the group of southern armies under the command of Marshal von Rundstedt, who rushed through the Ukraine, did not come to hardly six hundred tanks, a hardly believable figure!

Six hundred tanks to smash millions of Soviet soldiers, thousands of Soviet tanks, and to come, at the same time, to Rostov, at the very end of the Black Sea and the Sea of Azov, before winter arrived, without having diverted the essential plan of this fortified force to rush ahead and meet General Guderian coming down from the north in order to effect, along with him, the greatest encirclement in the military history of the world two hundred kilometres east of Kiev.

With five hundred more tanks the group of German invading armies in the south of the USSR would have reached Stalingrad and Baku before the onset of the cold. These tanks were missing, it was Mussolini who had caused them to be lost.

As catastrophic as this delay of five weeks in the schedule was, a more abundant German equipment would have, very probably, been able to compensate the imbalance in time. But, there too, the war began badly.

The information provided on the strength of the USSR was rapidly revealed to be false. The Soviets possessed not three thousand tanks, as the German secret services had claimed to Hitler, but ten thousand, that is to say, three times more tanks than Germany lined up. And certain types of Russian tanks, such as the T34 and the KV2 of fifty two tons, were normally invulnerable, of an extraordinary solidity, constructed quite especially to dominate the mud and the snow there.

Besides, the documentation on the ways of access through the Russian space was erroneous: great arteries that were envisaged for the tanks did not even exist; others, slushy, were just good enough to support the passage off light troikas. The slightest car would be submerged there.

Nevertheless, thanks to miracles of energy, the rush was accomplished. In twenty five days, seven hundred kilometres had been crossed and conquered. Already on 16 July 1941, Smolensk, the last big city on the highway that led to Moscow, had fallen. From the extreme point of the German advance, the loop of Elyna, there remained no more than 298 kilometres before reaching the capital of the USSR!

In two weeks of offensive at this rate this would have been attained. Stalin already prepared the transfer of the diplomatic corps to the other side of the Volga. Panic reigned. Demonstrations booed Communism. One even saw a swastika flag, fabricated in haste, wave in a street of Moscow.

But to rush to Moscow, of a relatively slight strategic interest, was to give up the destruction of the immense cohort of more than a million Soviet soldiers who, in the south, fled in disorder towards the Dniepr and towards the Dniester. One does not conduct a war to occupy cities but to destroy the combating force of the adversary.

These million Russians on the rout, were, left in peace, reconstituted in the background. Hitler was thus right. One should have taken them without any delay, with all their heavy equipment, in the trap of immense encirclements, compared to which the encirclements of Belgium and France in 1940 would be almost children's games. It would also have ensured economically, the enormous mineral wealth of the Donets.

Unfortuantely, Guderian did not have at his disposal sufficient forces to conduct, at the same time, the course towards Moscow and the destruction of the enemy at the other extremity of Russia. Whatever the choice may have been, the second operation would have almost certainly been engaged too late.

If, instead of having to stop one's tanks on the highway of Smolensk and abandon temporarily the conquest of Moscow, within reach, Hitler had at his disposal two or three thousand more tanks, the two gigantic operations, the conquest of Moscow in the east and the encirclement of the Soviet mass in the south, would have succeeded in time and at the same time. And even the third operation, the conquest, already before the winter of 1941, of the lower Volga and of the Caucasus.

For a long time one has been wondering how Hitler had been able to commit such an error of evaluation and throw himself across the gigantic empire of the Soviets with only 3254 tanks, more or less close to what he possessed when entering France in May 1940.

Had he too been victim of the illusions that distracted so many strategists following the pitiable military campaign of the Soviets in Finland during the winter of 1939–1940? No!

'When I gave the order to my troops to enter Russia', he told me one day, 'I had the feeling of breaking down with my shoulder a door behind which was an obscure locality of which I knew nothing!'

And then? . . . Then it was necessary to wait for the deployment of the archives of the Heereswaffenamt to know the reality. These documents reveal that, immediately after the campaign of France of 1940, Hitler, seeing the crushing Soviet threat confirmed, demanded a monthly production of *800 to 1000 tanks*. The figure was not foolish, and it was largely exceeded one year later. If the factories of the Reich had put out just a half of the tanks demanded by the Führer, the rush of Hitler tanks through the USSR would have been impossible to stop.

But, even at that time, the sabotage which ended in the assassination attempt against Hitler on 20 July 1944 was led underhandedly by important generals of the administration, to whom the production services had been secretly confided. Under pretext that these tanks would cost two billion marks (what of that?) and would require hundred thousand qualified workers (Germany was overflowing with them, the Wehrmacht being at that time inactive) the Heereswaffenamt smothered the production orders.

The saboteurs went even farther. Hitler had demanded that the III tanks, provided up to then with 37 calibre cannons, be endowed with 50mm L60 cannons, capable of overcoming the most powerful tanks. It was only at the end of winter, that is to say, too late that Hitler learnt that the cannons foreseen by him, 60 calibres in length, had only 42. This weakness proved to be fatal near Moscow.

'When Hitler noted in February 1942', Guderian recounts, 'that his instructions had not been executed, even though the technical possibilities existed, he was seized with a violent fury and never forgave the responsible officers for having acted on their own authority.'

But the damage had been done.

The effort of creation of new armament was almost insignificant. During these months the Third Reich, if it had really wanted it, could have easily produced five thousand, six thousand new tanks, more powerfully calibrated, adapted accurately to the climate and the extraordinary difficulties of the terrain that they had to encounter in their future combats.

Then, yes, the rush through the USSR would have been irresistible.

It was nothing of the sort. Twenty Pazer Divisions penetrated Russia on 22 June 1942 instead of the ten which had conquered Belgium, Holland and France in May of the preceding year. But the passage of ten to twenty divisions was theoretical. There were twice as many Panzer Divisions but twice fewer tanks in each of them.

In spite of everything, what happened is rather miraculous. Guderian descended with steady marches towards the Donets, conducting combats of unheard-of audacity. Two fabulous razzias, near Kieve, at Uman, where Guderian had not intervened, then near Poltava, destroyed the Soviet forces of the Dnieper. It was only after the latter encirclement, the most colossal of the war (665,000 prisoners, 884 tanks and 3718 cannons taken) that Hitler gave the order to Guderian to climb back to the north to try, not only to take Moscow from the back, that is to say, from the south-east, but even to penetrate as far as Nizhny-Novgorod (now Gorki) four hundred kilometres further east, on the Volga itself!

The operation, if it had succeeded, would have been the most miraculous tank cavalcade of all time: from Poland to Smolensk, then from Smolensk to Donets, then from Donets, again, towards to Moscow, and 80 leagues beyond that towards the Volga! Several thousands of kilometres to cross in five months, while combating! With worn out equipment, tired servants!

Guderian set off again across everything, accomplishing stages that reached upto twenty five kilometres a day. The same time as this, all the German tank forces of the north rushed towards Smolensk right in front of them, towards the Soviet capital. Moscow was going to be taken at the end of a manœuvre of a perfect strategic precision. The war would have ended after all!

The five weeks lost before the beginning of the campaign and the lack of two or three thousand tanks which would have permitted the doubling of the assault columns were going to make this immense final effort fail, *a few kilometres from success.*

From the end of October 1941, frightful slush had mired the tank formations of the Reich. Not a single tank advanced. No more cannon could be moved. The provisions remained stuck on the roads: not only the food of the soldiers but the munitions of the artillery and the petrol of the tanks. Ice would do the rest. It worsened, in November and the beginning of December 1941, in an increasingly catastrophic fashion, moving from $15°$ below zero, to $20°$ below zero, to $35°$ below zero, to reach even $50°$ below zero! For hundred and fifty years Russia had not seen a more ferocious winter!

It was impossible for the tanks to move. Forty percent of the soldiers had their feet frozen, deprived of the winter equipment which the supplies office had hardly thought of between 1940 and 1941. Still dressed in their light summer uniforms, without a coat and often without gloves, hardly nourished, they rushed inexorably to physical collapse.

Compared to them the Soviets had at their disposal tanks capable of braving the slush, ice and cold. The first English equipment had just reached the suburbs of Moscow. Fresh troops had been brought in, in a very large number, from Siberia, that a Japanese intervention — which also was deficient — had very usefully retained in Asia.

Each day the combat became more atrocious. However, the German assailants pursued their effort, whatever its rigour was. Some advance units even went past Moscow in the north to Krasnaya Polyana. Others had reached the suburbs of Moscow and occupied the tramway depot. Before them, in the devouring ice, the cupolas of the capital of the Soviets shone sprawling.

It was there, a few kilometres from the Kremlin itself, that the assault was checked forever. The units had become skeletal. The majority did not possess even a fifth of their numbers. The soldiers collapsed on the snow, incapable of the least effort. The weapons, frozen, were blocked, offered no service. The Soviets, on the contrary, buttressed hardly a few kilometres from their bases, received in abundance provisions, munitions and the support of new tanks that emerged in hundreds from the factories of Moscow itself. They were launched in a counter-offensive. The German survivors of this terrible epic were overwhelmend by the wave. The battle of Moscow was lost. Moreover, Stalin had won the semi-tranquillity of six months of winter, six months which would be an immediate rampart and his salvation later.

Chapter VIII
The Russian Inferno

Wherever one was, the drama was identically atrocious, from December 1941 to April 1942, over the three thousand kilometres extent of the Russian Front, from Petsamo[47] to the Sea of Azov. We, foreign volunteers, lost like the Germans in these frightful steppes, were reduced to the same extremities: having to die of the cold, die of hunger, and fight nevertheless.

My Belgian comrades and I were struggling at that time in the snows of Donets. Everywhere the howling cold wind. Everywhere howling enemies. The positions were cut out of blocks of ice. The orders were formal: do not retreat. The sufferings were inexpressible. Indescribable. The small horses that brought us frozen eggs, all grey, and weapons so cold that they burnt our fingers, sprinkled the snow with a blood that fell from their nostrils, drop by drop. The wounded were frozen, and fell down immediately. The limbs affected became, in two minutes, livid like parchment. Nobody risked urinating outside. Sometimes the jet itself was converted into a yellow curved stick. Thousands of soldiers had their sexual organs or anus atrophied forever. Our noses, ears were swollen like big apricots, from which a reddish and sticky pus flowed.

It was horrible, horrible. Just in our sector of the central ridge of the Donets more than eleven thousand wounded soldiers died in a few months in the miserable school where, cut off from everything by the snows which reached upto four metres high, military doctors, staggering with fatigue, amputated hundreds of feet and arms,

---

47 Petsamo was a northern Finnish province that was occupied by the Soviets during the battle of 1939–40 but returned by them to Finland in 1940.

stitched up torn stomachs contained in frozen blocks of blood and excrement, shining shells of reddish and greenish materials similar to tangled plants at the bottom of a petrified aquarium.

The evacuation, from our combat posts to this atrocious clinic, of these wounded exposed to the four winds, was made on the little carts of Russian peasants. The bodies were hardly protected by a little thatch torn off from the roofs of the last log cabins. The transfer lasted sometimes several days.

For a long time now the dead were no longer buried. One covered them in snow as one could. They would wait for the defrost to receive a grave. A raging vermin devoured us alive. In our dirty uniforms these grey lice with little shiny eggs like pearls were embedded one behind the other like grains of maize. One morning, in a fit of exasperation, I undressed in spite of the cold: I killed more than seven hundred of them on my body.

But our clothes themselves were no more than rags. Our underwear, become brownish, became frayed from week to week. It ended as emergency bandages for the wounded. Soldiers became mad, ran straight ahead, crying, into the endless snows. At every hand to hand combat, four, five, six men fled in this manner. The steppes quickly engulfed them. Never, I think, nowhere in the world, did so many men suffer so much.

In spite of everything they held fast. A general retreat through these interminable white and devouring deserts would have been a suicide. Hitler's refusal, sending to the devil his panicking generals who demanded a retreat of hundred, two hundred kilometres, saved the army, one cannot repeat that enough. In the cold of 40^0 and 50^0 below zero and under snow tornadoes which knocked everything down, what would a retreat have been able to lead to?

The majority of the men would have perished on the way, as the army of Napoleon perished, which did not march in mid-winter but in October and November, that is to say, in autumn. And Napoleon withdrew along a single highway axis and not back along three thousand kilometres of the front, through steppes drowned in a gigantic glacial mystery. However, of the hundreds of thousands of men that Napoleon had dragged with him in his retreat only a few thousands survived.

What then would have happened to the German troops drowned in a vastness of snow, in January and February 1942, at a time of the most terrible ice?

For a simple liaison operation, one day in January 1942, we needed seventeen hours to cross four kilometres, carving in the snow, with shovels and axes, a deep corridor.

The only snowplough provided to our sector had been blocked by walls of ice. It was impossible to break them in spite of furious efforts.

And even if we had been able, at the cost of the most terrible sufferings, to effect, in two or three weeks, a retreat of hundred or two hundred kilometres, what would have changed? Would there have been five centimetres less of snow? A large part of the army would have perished in retreating. The rest would have found itself in a more frightful situation, deprived of its last physical and moral force by such an effort, with less of its defensive equipment, having been left behind or abandoned on the way.

Hitler was right against these generals. It was necessary to bury ourselves no matter how, protect ourselves no matter how. Tolerate everything, bear everything, but survive! And even rush towards the enemy if, cut off from the back, one had to absolutely find a little food or a large dacha.

For they, the Russians, people of the snows, were not only physically cruder than us and were accustomed to the frightful cold of these climates, but they knew, for centuries, how to resist it. They possessed the art of fabricating shelters against the cold, more protective than our poor clumsily improvised refuges.

Some of their snow camps were semi-subterranean hamlets for Mongol tribes. The small nervous horses dwelt among these militarised muzhiks, strong, stocky, with eyes constricted through staring at the snow, their cheekbones yellow with the thick fat that they smeared themselves with and which warmed them.

Their feet, in their felt boots, were wound with large strips of wool. Their uniforms, double or triple, were sown on all sides, like swollen doughnuts. The cold wind did not penetrate them. They have lived in this way forever. And this particularly atrocious winter did not surprise them excessively. Protected in this way from the hostility of Nature, they could even engage in violent offensive operations, in the south as well as in the north.

We therefore had to counter-attack, retake the lost steppes. We reconquered destroyed villages. We carved out, before the blackened walls of the dachas, parapets of blocks of ice. Kilometres of snow separated our resistance groupings. The enemy infiltrated everywhere. The hand to hand combats were frightening.

In just one day, on 28 February 1942, in a destroyed village called Gromowaya-Balka (Valley of Thunder!), and where our battalion had been resisting the assault of four thousand Russians for a week, we lost in a frightful punch-up that lasted six hours from the morning to the night *half* of our comrades. We defended ourselves desperately among the corpses of horses on which the bullets resonated as on crystal. The Russians advanced in closed ranks, draped in their long violet coats. New waves surged endlessly which we cut down on frozen ponds.

That was how the Russian winter was. For seven months everything was a blinding white. The cold gnawed the bodies out. The combats filed down the last forces. Then, one morning, the sun appeared, fully red, above the white hills. The snows descended little by little down the high trees, crested by straw sheafs which had marked the trails until the day when these crested peaks had been submerged. Brownish waters hurtled down impetuously from all the hills, collected in the valleys. A mill began to turn in the blue sky. The Calvary of hundreds of millions of German and non-German soldiers of the Russian Front had ended. The tragedy of the winter had ended.

But it was the conquest of Russia that it was necessary to resume. The war tactics of Hitler was based not only on a new strategy — tanks and aerial strike force attacking together and in massed

The Russian inferno

formation — but also on the *effect of surprise*. In 1942 it would no longer be possible to count on this effect of surprise. Stalin knew this method already. The superiority of initiative was thus lost.

Hitler's strategic intervention had been a stroke of genius: the Blitzkrieg, that is to say, a lightning war, the stunning bursting into the back of the enemy, the massive breaking up of its lines, without any warning, at precise points where the essential part of the forces was deployed. The battering ram had been constituted of the enormous mass of tanks, before which the artillery of the stukas, sowing fear, broke everything into pieces and opened up pathways.

In Poland, Holland, the north of France, in Yugoslavia, this new formula of war had triumphed because, in each of these countries, it was the *first time* that it had been employed, permitting giant pincers, of iron and fire, to dive in and close down on the back of the adversary, who had been cornered, demoralised, annihilated in a trice. In a few days hundred thousand, two hundred thousand men were captured.

It is this same formula that Hitler had reedited in 1941 by bursting into Russia, effecting the same breakthroughs, the same catches, but at a fabulous level, notably in Ukraine and in the Donets. In four months, several million prisoners, thousands of cannons and tanks had been seized.

But the Ural was farther than the Pyrenees! One should have rushed there earlier. Or else been able, with a very superior force of tanks, to conduct two or three times the number of encirclement operations instead of having to run with the same forces, limited, from the north to the south and from the south to the north. The ice had gone ahead of Hitler, it had fallen on him with its forty or fifty degrees below zero, stronger than the steel of his armored divisions and the will of his audacious commanding officers. In 1942, it was therefore necessary to revise that, without counting any more on the fact that one could surprise an enemy now warned in advance.

Besides, Stalin, who also was a genius in his way, an elementary genius, who plunged his will every day in the blood of others in order to revive it, had had the time not only to detect the secrets of the Hitlerian strategy which had almost broken him but to find a response to it. It was simple: gain time; gain months, years, during which he could form new armies, draw, without any pity, from the reservoir of the two hundred million inhabitants of the USSR, forge in his turn dozens of tank divisions which, one day, would outstrip in a crushing fashion — twenty thousand tanks against a few thousands — the armored divisions which had ensured the devastating triumphs of Hitler, from autumn 1939 to autumn 1942.

Hitler, in the summer of 1942, still reaped very spectacular victories between the Don, the Volga and the Caucasus. But the efforts at large encirclements did not succeed any longer. Like the bull that cannot be surprised twice, the Russians had detected the traps and avoided them in time every time.

The last Soviet error was committed in May 1942. And it succeeded in putting Stalin on guard. His troops had given themselves the luxury of taking the initiative prematurely. Perhaps they sought to disorganise the German offensive mass which was preparing to gain its impetus in the south? In any case, we were, in the first days of May 1942, on the verge of being submerged, in the Donets, by the enormous avalanche of Soviet troops surging from the region of Kharkov towards the Dnieper and Dnipropetrovsk.

They knocked down the German front, rushed forward. But they rushed without any result.

Rushing is not sufficient to destroy. The Russians had not yet exactly seized the mechanism of pincers of encirclement. We let them get lost in the emptiness. The German divisions and the foreign volunteers, Belgian, Hungarian, Romanian, Croatian, Italian, did not panic. All remained exactly stuck to the flanks of the enemy opening.

They closed in at the back when they were knocked out too far and in a primitive fashion. Again, as in 1941, hundreds of thousands of Russians were made prisoners. None of their units could escape. We were massed on the two sides and on the back of the Soviet army caught in our trap.

The Russian inferno

It was a great disaster for the Russians that Hitler completed by taking advantage of this terrible bloodbath of the Soviets to throw himself on Orel, opening in this way to his troops the route of the plains of the Don, of Stalingrad and the Caucasus.

Stalin was definitively aware that he was far from equalling his victor tactically. He would no longer risk attacking him extensively before his forces had become superior to those of the Reich.

So they could compensate only through numbers the tactical superiority of the tank armies of Hitler, still devastating in the spring of 1942, but which were thinned down as the young leaders of the Red Army, detached from the routine ignorance of their elders, assimilated in time, through tenacity and also through setbacks that were intelligently analysed, the strategy that had made Hitler the victor and which would end by turning him into the defeated.

One could believe, in the summer of 1942, that Hitler, throwing himself towards the southern extremity of Soviet Russia was going this time to finish the Russian colossus for good. The breaches of July and August 1942 had been absolutely impressive.

We ourselves who participated in it were thrilled. We rode across the magnificent plains of the Don, where millions of maize and sunflower plants, three metres tall, extended to the golden horizon. We crossed by swimming, Tommy guns on our back, the green rivers, one kilometre wide, at the foot of hills mounted with antique Tartar tombs and decorated with branches of ripening grapes. We advanced thirty, forty kilometres every day. In a few weeks the left wing of the offensive had arrived close to Stalingrad.

On the right wing, we had crossed the Don, reached the large lakes of Manych, starry in the night with millions of unreal daisies thrown by the moon on the waves. Some camels outlined their bald humps frayed like old leather.

A whirlwind of dust, dozens of kilometres long, signalled columns of tanks that thousands of young infantrymen followed with collars open singing at the top of their voices in the burning summer. At the beginning of August, beyond the leaping waters of the Kuban river, the giant peaks of the Caucasus rose before our dazzled eyes, with white summits brilliant as glass. In the clearings of the first forests, before some wooden huts perched on stilts — to protect them from wolves in the winter — some Armenian women milked giant buffaloes with necks hanging like grey boas. We had advanced more than a thousand kilometres! We had arrived at the frontiers of Asia! Who would stop us now?

However, in reality, we had not arrived anywhere, for, if we had conquered the land, we had not seized the adversary by the neck. The latter had fled before being caught in our encirclements. Everywhere he had disappeared. We even thought that he did not exist. He would brace himself on the ground only when we had arrived almost at the end of our course, terribly far from our bases, reduced in numbers: wounded, crippled, men sick with dysentery had been left behind on the way, very many.

The summer was going to end. It was only then that the Russians turned round, at the moment that the first rains of autumn beat down in big buckets. Was the Russian winter going to stop everything a second time? Cause us to mess everything up?

Lucid, having finally understood that a bloodbath similar to that of 1941 would complete his loss, Stalin had taken extreme care not to let his troops any longer be caught anywhere. It would be better for him to lose thousand kilometres than five million men, as in the preceding year. Space, during war, is like an accordion. It goes and comes back.

We had succeeded in conquering only the golden air of summer and a scorched earth. The rails of the railways had been cut through every ten metres. The factories had been emptied of their materials to the last workbench and the last bolt. The coal mines burned everywhere, fantastic masses of orange that made our horses crazy.

In the villages there remained only some old peasants, quite bent, pious and meek peasant women, beautiful little blond boys playing near wooden wells. In the public squares only the horrible statues, always the same, of common cement, of a Lenin in a petty bourgeois jacket and with Asiatic eyes, or of a buxom sportswoman with massive thighs like concrete logs.

The only serious resistance we encountered too late, at the very end, just at the moment when one should have concluded the conquest by removing the petroleum wells in front of the border of Persia — the real objective of our offensive towards the south — whereas Paulus should have definitively pushed back the Russians from the other side of the Volga, which had become the border of Europe. But there also the Soviets had suddenly bolstered themselves.

I experienced, like so many others, the desperate effort of these last weeks, these weeks when we felt, for the first time, that, perhaps, victory, that is to say, Russia, had eluded us. We had reached hundred kilometres from Turkic Asia, with high and wild mountains, forests of virgin oaks, where one could advance only with blows of the axe, riddled with obstacles, drenched by the autumn rains. The tanks did not go through any more. The animals did not go through any more, or they died of hunger, beaten by the gusts of wind.

We wove our way with great difficulty through these spongy forests, with eternal vegetation, closed with thick and thorny bushes of thousands of wild blackthorn. There the Russians were kings, having prepared their lair much in advance, watchful in the thick bushes, or positioned astride the branches of the enormous forest. They offered us a thousand traps, pelted us, invisible, present everywhere.

The rains, mixed with the first snows, beat like a hurricane. They cut off, before our backs, the timber bridges that we had thrown down on the streams during our advance. It was through them alone that some makeshift food supplies and some ammunition could still reach us. Reduced to ourselves we lived on the raw meat of horses that had died a week or two before and that the overflowing waters had thrown on the bends of the rivers. We reduced them with our knives into a sort of blackish mash.

Jaundice transformed the soldiers into ghosts: in our sector alone, near Adler and Tuapse, twelve thousand jaundiced men were evacuated in a week. Our legion, like many other units, was only a shadow of itself, reduced to a seventh of its numbers! Emaciated, we were perched at a height of more than thousand metres on peaks swept by tempests, under trees twisted by autumnal tornadoes. The Russians climbed in the night from tree stump to tree stump upto our dens inundated with water which pierced the line of our ridge. We let them approach upto two or three metres. In the shade we engaged in atrocious combats. The barrages during the day were such that the corpses, at night, had to remain hitched to roots in the open air until the head was detached at the end of two or three weeks and there remained before our distraught eyes only grey vertebrae sticking out of jackets, superposed one on top of the other like the necklaces of negresses.

Few of us had not been wounded. I had my stomach punctured and liver peforated. What else could I have done but remain among my men on the verge of a breakdown? We were only human wrecks now, starving, hirsute. How, in this condition, would we spend a second winter when the snows would have covered the entire mountain chain and the entire hinterland?

It was then, on 19 November 1942, at five in the morning, at the other end of the Southern front, in the north-west of Stalingrad, at the bridgehead of Kremenskaya, on the Don, that thousands of Soviet cannons roared, that thousands of tanks threw themselves across the positions of the Third and Fourth Romanian armies.

One week later, two hundred and thirty thousand German soldiers would be thrown back towards Stalingrad in an encirclement which was in reality no more serious than twenty encirclements where the Russians had been caught previously, which could even have been broken, but which the incompetence and apathy of the fussy functionary that General Paulus was converted in a few weeks into a disaster. The Second World War had reached its great breaking point. The invincible Germany of Hitler had been defeated for the first time. It had just toppled over on the slope of defeat. The fall was prolonged for almost one thousand days before the last corpse, that of Hitler, was burnt in Berlin, under two hundred litres of petrol, in the blackened garden of the Chancellery.

Léon Degrelle speaks at an early REX meeting.

In 1936, the Parti Rexiste won 21 deputies and 12 senators in the Belgian parliament, becoming one of the larger parties.

In 1941, Degrelle led a recruiting drive for Belgian volunteers to take part in the European crusade against the Soviet Union. Here he speaks at a recruiting rally in front of a portrait of Adolf Hitler.

A Walloon SS rally, 1942.

Volunteers also came from the Flemish-speaking region of Belgium: A Flemish SS rally in 1942.

A Walloon SS recruiting poster.

Photographs

Walloon SS (note the Belgian flag on the sleeve of the soldier on the right) on the Eastern Front.

Degrelle receives the Knight's Cross from Hitler, 1943.

Back in Brussels, Degrelle hands out medals to Walloon SS Eastsen Front veterans, 1944.

Degrelle reviews the Walloon SS parade in Brussels, 1944.

A postcard made from the Walloon SS parade in Brussels, 1944. Degrelle salutes his troops as two of his children look on.

Degrelle featured in the German army magazine Signal, 1944.

The Heinkel He 111 on which Degrelle escaped to Spain, as it crash-landed on the beach, May 1945.

Degrelle photographed in dress uniform, Spain, after the war.

Chapter IX
Who Was Hitler?

This Hitler, of whom nobody knows exactly, dozens of years later, if his charred remains still exist, and where they could have ended up, who was he? What was this man who shattered the world and changed its destiny forever? What was his character? What were his passions? What did he think? What took place in his heart? Did he have one? And what was his internal thought-process until the day when, just a few hundred metres from the triumphant Russians, he blew his brains out?

I knew him, knew him for ten years, knew him from close quarters at the moment of his glory, as at the moment when, around him, the universe of his works and his dreams collapsed. I know. I know who he was: the political leader, the war leader, the man, the man himself.

It is really too simple to be satisfied with covering with outrages the skin of a dead defeated man, with saying, writing, inventing anything at all about him certain that the public will accept anything provided that it completes the idea that it has formed of Hitler — that of a monster! — certain also of the fact that the rare witnesses who could explain that he was not that will remain silent in order not to be enclosed immediately in the same ignominious bag as the dead Hitler.

Everything that the public can recount, or everything that one could recount to it, leaves me perfectly indifferent. What is important is the truth, which is what I know. Besides, it requires the imbecility of the masses to believe that a man who drew hundred million Germans behind him, for whom millions of young men died, was only a sort of Sardanapalus or Nero, drinking blood from morning to night from the tap of his folly.

I can still see him in Berlin on 1 May 1943 perched at the summit of a grand rostrum on the Tempelhof airfield. Hundreds of thousands of spectators rumbled with fervour under his look. However, I had been disappointed. His eloquence was not very nuanced, violent, basic, rather monotone. A Latin public would have been more demanding. Even the irony was rough. It was a forced eloquence more than an artistic eloquence.

Similarly, the brilliance of his eyes never impressed me particularly. They did not penetrate, as they say, the look of the interlocutor. Their fire did not have anything unbearable about them. Blue, bright, the eyes were beautiful, their glow was powerful certainly, but they did not seek either to intimidate or to seduce, nor, especially, to cajole. One could indeed look him in the face intensely, without feeling that you were being invaded or that he was being disturbed.

Similarly regarding the famous currents. Crazy old women like Princess Hélène of Romania have written that when Hitler shook your hand his fingers emitted electrical discharges, evidently diabolical! Hitler did not shake hands very much, they were rather soft. Generally, especially with true friends, Hitler did not offer his hand but pressed your hand within his hands. I never felt pierced by this touch like the old crazy Romanian princess. Never did I jump into the air with a burning sensation! It was a very ordinary fist like that of a forest guard of the Ardennes.

Hitler was simple, very well groomed. His ears always astonished me, gleaming like shells. He did not act like a playboy, believe me. His clothes were ironed carefully, it is difficult to say more. His military jackets were all the same, without any grace. His shoe size was 43: one night when I had arrived at his place shod in boots of Russian felt, he went to his closet, brought me a pair of his own boots and shoved into a corner a piece of newspaper so that I would not float in them, for my shoe-size was 42. This detail shows you how uncomplicated the man was.

Who was Hitler?

He needed nothing, except beauty. He bought, with the royalties of his *Mein Kampf* a marvellous Botticelli which he hung just above his bed. He died without leaving behind a single penny. For him, this problem of personal goods, of personal money, did not even exist. I am sure that, during the last years of his life, he did not think of them a single time.

He ate in ten minutes. And even his meal was a rather surprising spectacle. For this man who slept at five or six in the morning every day, and who was already up at eleven, spectactles in his hand, before his files, hardly ate. And then it was dishes that for most people 'do not supply strength'. He conducted the entire terrible effort of the war without having swallowed even once hundred grams of meat. He did not eat eggs. He did not eat fish. A plate of pasta or a plate of vegetables. Some cakes. Some water. Always water. And the Hitlerian culinary festivities were ended!

He had a passion for music. Even to a stupefying degree. He had an auditory memory worthy of the spoken-word memory of de Gaulle. A musical motif, heard by him one time, was absorbed forever. He whistled it without a mistake, no matter how long it was. Wagner was his god. He did not miss a single nuance of him. He confused, in Spanish history, Isabel the Catholic (XV century) and Isabel II (XIX century), but he would not have confused two notes of the entire musical repertory of the entire world.

He loved his dog. During the First World War somebody had stolen a dog from him. This was one of the greatest sorrows of his youth. Yes, that's how it was. I knew Blondie, his dog of the last years. The good animal paced alongside him the floorboards of his bunker, as if it too was aware of the tragic eventualities of the Russian Front. Hitler prepared his feed for him himself around midnight, leaving the visitors who were present to go and feed his companion.

And female companions? There, truly, people have exceeded all limits of the imagination concerning madness, or even sadism. If there was ever a man for whom the love of women counted little, it is Hitler.

He never spoke of women. He had a horror of guardroom jokes of which so many men — small natures especially — are gourmands. I shall go further: he was a prude. A prude especially in his clothes. A prude in his feelings.

He admired feminine beauty. One day, he was furious because his officer had not asked a young girl, extraordinarily beautiful and radiant, who had thrown herself on his car to acclaim him, for her address. Not that he would have made a date, as hundred men would have done, but he would have loved to send her a bouquet of flowers.

He liked female company. I knew very well Sigrid von Weldseck, the very prettiest young woman of the Reich, tall, with bright eyes, marvellously soft skin, slight breasts. Anybody would have been mad in love with her. I spent the last fine hours of the war with her, in fact when, in my sector of the Oder Front, she came to look for the bundle of letters that her friend the Führer had written to her.

Oh well! the essential part of their relations consisted, she herself recounted it to me, in going to his place every Tuesday — and she did not even go there alone — in order to be enchanted by music! Hitler did not abound in secrets about his female successes. Millions of German women — and non-German! — were in love with him. An entire cupboard enclosed letters from women who had begged him to bear their child! He did not even pay court to them. I would add that he did not value love at all. A frightening fatality marked his diverse sentimental desires.

He had begun with an innocent love. The heroine was called Stefanie. She was sixteen. Every evening he installed himself on the Linz bridge to see her pass. Oh well! never, during the months that his relationship lasted, did he dare to tell her a word. Hitler — that seemed unthinkable — was a shy person. But shy like a communicant girl. He consumed himself for two years in loving this Stefanie from afar. He sketched the palace, Wagnerian of course, where they would live happily. He wrote to her, from Vienna, passionate letters, in nervous, hatched characters. But the signature was illegible, and the address was not indicated.

Who was Hitler?

'It's true, I remember. But that is from a long time ago! Fifty years! Yes, I did receive the letters that you mention. But, if I understand you right, these were letters from Hitler?' It's Stefanie speaking. Never did her lover of that time dare to introduce himself. She got married. She lived in Vienna, a very old lady, widow of a lieutenant-colonel. This was Hitler's first love. At twenty, entirely absorbed by this dumb love, Hitler was still a virgin. That was how it was. It is true, strictly true.

Obviously people have recounted hundred imbecile stories about the loves of Hitler, with Viennese prostitutes, with Jewesses, obviously, and even about the syphilis that these women had gifted him. These are lies. In his entire youth, there was only one love, that of Stefanie. And he never spoke a word to her.

If the love for Stefanie did not end in anything, all the other loves of Hitler ended only in catastrophes. Not a single one of the women who held the man in their arms who was certainly the most beloved in Europe ended her novel without a horrifying drama. The first hanged herself in a hotel room. The second, his niece Geli,[48] killed herself in his apartment in Munich, with his own revolver. Hitler was maddened by this. For three days, he paced about his little Bavarian apartment ready to commit suicide. Never again did the memory of Geli leave his life. Geli was everywhere. Her bust was endlessly adorned with flowers. The third was Eva Braun, Eva Braun, around whom people have woven fabulous legends, often, nonsensical, sometimes grotesque.

Here too I was a witness. I knew everything about her. She was a little employee of Hitler's best friend, the Munich photographer Hoffmann,[49] a very good friend of mine equally. She was madly in love with the handsome Adolf, even if badly dressed at that time,

---

[48] Geli Raubal (1908–1931) was Hitler's half-niece, of whom he was very possessive. When he discovered, in 1927, that she was having an affair with his chauffeur Emil Maurice, he dismissed the latter from his service. She committed suicide in September 1931.

[49] Heinrich Hoffmann (1885–1957) was Hitler's official photographer. He published many illustrated books of Hitler's accomplishments during the Reich, as well as his own memoirs, called *Hitler was my friend* (tr. R.H. Stevens), London, 1955.

in his frightful light-coloured gabardine, always crumpled, his hair falling like the tail of a dead bird, his rather large nose, supported by the little toothbrush of his moustache.

But the beautiful Eva, plump and pink, loved him to madness. She tried to trap him with a kiss. One New Year's night, she persuaded Hoffmann, her boss, to phone him so that he might join them in their celebration. He did not go out often. Even New Year's night he spent alone in his two-room apartment. He was finally persuaded and arrived.

Just at the moment when he walked, without noticing it, under the mistletoe, the beautiful Eva, who was lying in wait for the moment, jumped on his neck, following the old custom. Hitler stopped suddenly, blushed like a conscript, turned on his heels, snatched his gabardine from the coat rack and rushed out onto the street, without having unclenched his teeth. I tell you: with regard to women he was incredibly shy. A single kiss had caused to flee the one who caused the whole of Europe to flee, ten years later!

But the affair was not to stand there. The poor Eva was more in love than ever. Then, once again, drama entered. When she was fully aware that her dear Adolf was radically inaccessible, she also took a small revolver and fired it right into her heart.

One generally does not know about this suicide attempt. But ten years before committing suicide in Berlin, next to Hitler, Eva Braun had already wanted, for love of Hitler, to commit suicide a first time, in Munich. After the two preceding corpses, it was something to be afraid of. Eva was not dead. Hitler wanted to know if it was really a suicide to die or, simply, to impress him with a little drama.

The report of the professor from the University of Munich who, at his request, examined her, was categorical. Eva had missed death only by a few millimetres. She had indeed been the complete mistress, the one who preferred to die rather than to not be able to project towards her beloved the full extent of her life.

It is from that time that Eva Braun entered Hitler's life. Oh! a discreet entry. One never saw them alone. She had been invited to

Berchtesgaden, but always in the company of other young women of those who worked with the Führer. They sat in the sun, on the terrace, in front of the grey, blue and white Alps, there was never a friendship — for it was, especially, a friendship — more reserved than this love. All the fairy tales about them are the works of total fantasy. Hitler adored children, received them on his terrace, cajoled them. But he never had any of Eva, or of any other woman. In his life, woman was never anything but a flash of beauty, among the works of his political life, which was *everything* for him. And further, the shades of death always darkened the fugitive light of the feminine face on which his gaze fell.

For that was not the end of the revolver bullets. Another feminine crackle of fire was going to resound under Hitler's balcony on the first day of the Second World War. This time it was an Englishwoman who committed suicide. She was a marvellous girl. I knew her well and admired her, as well as her sisters, of whom one was the wife of Oswald Mosley, the leader of the English Fascists. All were beautiful but Unity — Unity Mitford — was like a Greek goddess, slender, blonde, the perfect Germanic type. She had imagined that Hitler and she could incarnate the Germano-British alliance of which Hitler always dreamed, that he evoked again some days before dying. Unity followed Hitler everywhere.

When the latter crossed through crowds before reaching the podium she was there, radiant, transfigured. Every time a tender smile lit Hitler's rough face, for a brief instant. For, if Hitler admired, stroked with his look with a certain emotion, the admirable face and perfect body of Unity, notably in the house of Wagner in Bayreuth, the idyll was always limited to that. Hitler was at that time on the eve of the war, and the golden hair of the beautiful Unity could not easily become his exclusive preoccupation.

But for Unity, Hitler was everything. When, on the 3 September 1939, war with England broke out and Unity understood that her love would be torn apart, she walked beyond the rose beds that blossomed under the windows of the Führer and took out her revolver from her handbag. The bullet wounded her seriously in the head but did not kill her. Then something extraordinary happened.

After Hitler had confided her to the best surgeons of the Reich, who saved her (every day he had roses sent to her during the thick of the war with Poland), he organised her return to Great Britain.

Now, it was the winter of 1939–1940, and already the principal countries of the continent had entered into the conflict. However, Hitler arranged that a special train would transport the wounded woman, not only through Switzerland but through all of the French territory upto Dunkirk, when a ship, with the Luftwaffe flying over and protecting it, brought her to the shores of her country. It was no use. Unity survived during the hostilities, ravaged by her pain. Then she died, after Hitler's body had disappeared in the conflagration in the garden of the Chancellery on 30 April 1945.

There was thus nobody but Eva from 1939. Her role remained very modest upto the end. I say that because I spent almost an entire week at Hitler's during those years, in his large general headquarters.

Eva Braun never appeared there. Never, besides, did a single woman, whoever she may have been, share Hitler's intimacy during the four years that he spent, cloistered, in his buildings behind the front. Eva wrote. She phoned in the evening, around 10 o'clock. This quiet love-affair, as discreet as it was romantic, was limited to that. Only the end of the war brought it to a grandiose conclusion. When Eva took stock of everything that had happened, that the man whom she loved more than everything was going to succumb, she flew to the furnace of Berlin in order to be able to die at his side.

It was then, on the very last day of his existence, to honour in her the courage of German woman and the sacrifice of the mistress who preferred to die rather than to survive the one whom she loved, that Hitler married her. Before, he had not married, because his wife, his ony wife, was *Germany*. That day, he left Germany forever. He therefore married Eva. It was really a homage. His last night too he did not spend with her. He was the wise hero. He remained that upto the brink of death. Everything was tragic upto the end. When, beside the burning body of Hitler bathed in petrol, the body of Eva began to crackle its torso suddenly became erect. There was a frightening second. Then it fell again into the flames. In this way was consumed the last love of Adolf Hitler.

As hallucinating as the sentimental life — so little known — of the leader of the Third Reich was, it occupied, in reality, a rather insignificant part of his existence. What mattered for him, really, exclusively, was his public fight. Politically never did any man in the world raise a people up as Hitler did. But anyone who could now discover among the large German public an ex-Hitlerian who proclaims himself fearlessly would be quite clever!

The truth, however, is that almost all the Germans were Hitlerians, from the beginning, or later. Every election, every referendum, brought to him a simmering, and finally almost unanimous, adherence. The people voted for him because they wanted to vote for him. Nobody forced them to it. Nobody controlled them. Whether on the territory of the Reich itself or in the regions still subject to foreign authorities (Sarre, Danzig, Memel) the results were identical. To say the contrary is wrong. In every election the German people proved that they were basically with its Führer. And why would they not have been?

Hitler had raised them from economic stagnation. He had put back to work millions of desperate unemployed. Hundred new social laws had guaranteed the work, health, leisure-time, honour, of the workers. Hitler had invented for them the popular car, the Volkswagen, payable at a low price over several years. His holiday ships conducted thousands of workers from the fjords of Norway to the Canaries.

He had revivified the industry of the Reich, which had become the most modern and efficient of the continent. He had gifted Germany — a quarter century before France tried to imitate it — splendid highways. He had reunified the nation, given an army to a country that did not have a right any longer to possess tanks or cannons. A defeated country bled white (three million dead!) by the First World War he had transformed into the strongest country of Europe.

But above all — and that has been quite forgotten, now, it was the principal accomplishment of Hitler, the one that politically changed Europe — he had reconciled the mass of working people to the fatherland. International Marxism — and diverse cosmopolitan influences — had, in fifty years, separated the people from the nation everywhere. The Red worker was against the fatherland, not without reason always, for the fatherland of the rich had often been a stepmother to him.

In Belgium, he marched behind Red flags with broken rifles. In France, the military rebellions of Marty had been his work. In Germany, the Communists tore off the epaulettes of the officers. The fatherland was the bourgeoisie. Marxism was the anti-fatherland.

Hitler, thanks to his revolutionary programme of social justice and thanks to the immense improvement that he brought to the life of the workers, brought millions of proletarians to the national idea, notably six million of German Communists, who seemd lost forever to their fatherland, who were even its saboteurs, and could have become its gravediggers.

The true victory — a durable victory and of definitive scope — that Hitler won over Marxism was this: the reconciliation of nationalism with socialism, whence the name National Socialism, in fact the finest name that any party in the world could ever have borne. With the love of the native land, which was normal but left to itself would be too narrow, he united the universal spirit of socialism, bringing, not in words, but into real life, social justice and respect for the workers. Nationalism was too often, before Hitler, the exclusive domain of the bourgeoisie and the middle classes. At the opposite end, socialism was the almost exclusive domain of the working class alone. Hitler made a synthesis of the two. Is an aging de Gaulle trying anything different?

Where the acts of Hitler are least known is in the domain of war strategy. Apart from Cartier, who in his book *Les Secrets de la guerre dévoilés à Nuremberg* has established, supported by documents, the breadth of the military genius of the Führer, it is fashionable among the minds that think themselves distinguished to speak with an ironic condescendence of Hitler's interventions in the war operations of his time. However it is Raymond Cartier who is right.

The most sensational thing about Hitler was — and history will indeed recognise it one day — his military genius. An eminently creative genius. A stunning genius. The invention of modern strategy was his work. His generals applied, with more or less conviction, his instructions. But, left to themselves, they would not have been worth more than the French and Italian generals of their generation. They were, like them, of an older war, having hardly detected, before 1939, the importance of the combined action of airforce and tanks that Hitler obliged them to employ.

Even de Gaulle, who is a pioneer figure in this domain, was that only partially. He understood that the breaks of the front would never be obtained by scattering the combat tanks, battalion by battalion, with common cannons, with limited support. In that he knocked down the outdated theories of the French general staff. By contrast, what de Gaulle did not understand and Hitler did with a vivacity of a genius was the indispensable combination of land assault — by means of the mass of tanks surging at a precise point — and of the simultaneous aerial assault of squadrons of planes attacking in crushing waves the fixed point of breaks, crushing everything, opening a hole. Without the Stukas, the break of the Panzer Divisions at Sedan, on 13 May 1940, would not have been possible. It was the massive fall of thousand Stukas on the left bank of the Meuse that forced opened a path.

Some German military men understood remarkably, from the beginning, from 1934, the importance of the new strategy that Hitler explained to them, the Guderians, for example, the Rommels, the Mansteins. But, to tell the truth, they were officers who were little known, even little important. They were also discovered by Hitler, who, sensing that they were receptive, pushied them forward, provided them with orders and the instruments. They were only a handful. The mass of German generals, recalcitrant or little convinced of these novelties, remained, upto 1940, specialists highly qualified in an outdated strategy which would not have in any way permitted the conquest in three weeks of the whole of Poland, nor especially the fabulous motorised cavalcade from Sedan to Nantes and Lyon, in May and June 1940.

Hitler was, militarily, an inventor. People still talk of errors that he may have committed. The extraordinary thing would have been that, obliged to invent constantly, he did not commit any. But he invented, besides the strategy of motorised regrouping of land forces and air forces — which one would teach in military schools all over the world –, also operations that were totally diverse, such as the landing in Norway, the conquest of Crete, the adaptation of tank warfare to the sands of Africa of which nobody had thought upto then — and, even, also, airlifts. That of Stalingrad was difficult, complicated and perilous in a different way from that of the Americans in Berlin ten years later.

Hitler knew each detail of the motors, every advantage or disadvantage of the pieces of artillery, every type of submarine or ship, and the composition of the navy of every country. His knowledge and his memory regarding all these chapters was prodigious. Nobody caught him off guard. He knew about these thousand times more than his best specialists.

Further, it was necessary to possess strength of will. He had that always, to a supreme degree. Politically, only his steel will broke all the obstacles, made him conquer the extraordinary difficulties that would have broken any other man. It brought him to power in an absolute respect for the laws, recognised legitimately by the Reichstag, where his party, with the most numbers in the Reich, was still, however, a minority the day Marshal Hindenbug appointed him Chancellor.

Strength and ruse. Hitler was clever, crafty. And also cheerful. He has been depicted as a wild brute, rolling in fury on the floorboards, biting the carpet with his canines. Between ourselves, I do not know really how this mandibular exploit would have been possible! I spent many days and many nights close to Hitler. Never did I witness one of these furies that have been described so many times.

That there might have been a few of these is certainly not impossible. What man, bearing on his shoulders thousand times less care than Hitler, has never blown off his top? Who is the husband who has not made noisy scenes with his wife, who has not slammed the doors, who has not broken a dish or two? . . . That Hitler sometimes mounted his high horse is not improbable. So much more that causes of irritation were not lacking: imbecile generals who did not understand anything, who withdrew, who did not obey at all, who sabotaged orders, collaborators who lied; a rhythm of production that was not maintained; setbacks that appeared from all sides; fatal betrayals within his immediate entourage. But, even then, Hitler was capable of remaining perfectly calm.

I remember a quite typical case. One afternoon, in the autumn of 1944, I was at Hitler's, where I had just arrived with Himmler in his long green car. We were taking tea when, suddenly, a stupefying piece of news fell on us: the British airborne divisions had just been parachuted with complete success in Holland, just behind the Germans, at Arnheim, near Nimègue. It was the entire system of the western defence attacked from behind, and the access to the Ruhr threatened in an immediate and direct manner!

It has been recounted, later, complacently that a Dutch traitor of the Resistance had, in advance, informed the Germans of this plan. Which would have allowed the annihilation in a few days of these British divisions. This is a lie, one more lie, like so many others that were thrown up after 1945. I can say that because I was there when the news was announced to Hitler and Himmler. It struck them dumbfounded. But I saw also what happened thereafter: Hitler, regaining his composure in two minutes, convoking his general staff, analysing the situation for two hours, thinking of the facts of the case, then, in the general silence, dictating his orders, slowly, without any rise in his voice. It was impeccable and magnificent. He stopped. He asked that they bring him some hot tea. And, having closed the subject of the war, he spoke to me, until the night, about liberalism! I assure you that he had not eaten the carpet that afternoon with his teeth! He even made some jokes, then left, calm, slightly bent, to walk under the pines with Blondie his dog.

Not only were these stories of the extreme fury of Hitler rather fabulous, but he was a delicate man, full of attentions. I have seen him prepare sandwiches himself for one of his collaborators who was leaving on a mission. One night when I was discussing matters with Marshal Keitel in a shack, he, the abstemious, appeared bearing a bottle of champagne to cheer up our conversation.

Contrarily to everything that people have said, he was a moderate. As regards the religious point of view, he had his own positions. He could not tolerate the political interventions of the clergy, which was not reprehensible in itself. What was impressive, on the contrary, was his idea of the future of religions.

In his eyes, it had become useless to combat them, persecute them: the discoveries of science, dissipating the mysteries — essential for the influence of the Churches — and the progress of comfort — chasing away a misery which, for two thousand years, brought to the Church so many unfortunate beings — would, in his opinion, increasingly reduce the influence of religions.

'At the end of two centuries, three centuries' he told me, 'they will have arrived, some at extinction, others at an almost total depletion'.

One should say that the crisis, during the last years, of all the religions and especially of the Catholic religion, its reduction, or its elimination among the coloured peoples, its forced imposition on white Europe, its doctrinal 'adaptations', its retreat before Judaism which had been treated upto then as a millennial enemy and which it formerly sent so cheerfully to the stake, its late demagogy, its discipinary devaluations, its outbreaks of anarchy and doubtful fantasies, have not especially proven Hitler wrong. His view of this development, unimaginable at that time, also had, if one may say so, been prophetic.

The practice of religion did not disturb him. I had obtained from him that our Catholic chaplains might pursue their calling among our soldiers after we had become a brigade and then a division of the Waffen SS. Our example created a ripple effect. The most original figure of the French division of the Waffen SS, the Charlemagne, was a Catholic prelate, Monseigneur Mayol de Lupé, a coloured colossus, commander of the Legion of Honour and Iron Cross, first class. This prelate of His Holiness (an HH!)[50] did not disturb Hitler in any way, neither did our manner of practising our religion.

One morning when, staying at Hitler's, I went, more pious than today, to attend mass, I chanced upon him in a fir-tree lined alley. He was going to go to bed, finishing his day early in the morning. I was beginning mine. We wished each other good night and good day. Then, suddenly, he raised his nose, which was quite thick, towards me: 'But Léon, where are you going at this hour?' — 'I am going to communion', I replied to him directly. A gleam of surprise emerged from his eyes. Then he told me, affectionately: 'Oh well, truly, if my mother were still alive, she would have accompanied you.'

With him I never felt the object of the least discredit, the least suspicion because I was a Catholic. Many times I even repeated to Hitler that, after the war, as soon as I set foot again in my country, I would leave politics to assist in the moral and spiritual flourishing of the new European complex. 'Politics is one sector. It is not the only one. Souls should also have their own life and flourish. It is necessary that the new Europe render this flourishing possible, easy and free.'

In any case, it was upto the Christians to raise their ideal high in the new world that was beginning. Even if certain of the leading principles of the Third Reich were hostile to their religious convictions, they should hold their ground, exactly as the believers had done under Bismarck as well as under the French Republic of Combes.[51] They had not deserted their political responsibilities under regimes which, however, had expelled priests from the convents or imposed secular schools. In all, one fights only by being *present*, by throwing oneself into the fray as strongly as possible, instead of moaning in a sterile way in the distance.

---

50 In the French original, His Holiness (Sa Sainteté) lends itself to the pun 'another SS'.
51 Émile Combes (1835–1921) was a Socialist politician and Freemason who served as French Prime Minister from 1902–1905.

Hitler was as he was. The genius has his excesses. But he also has extraordinary powers of creation and divination. Hitler the conqueror would have been able to bring to Europe, unified by arms, considerable possibilities. But also, unquestionably, considerable dangers. To exploit the former and to exorcise the latter, the best would still have been to be installed solidly in one's place. That was, in any case, my choice. Shunning the victorious Third Reich in its entirety (and it could have been the victor, the large majority of Europeans certainly believed, in 1940 and in 1941, that it was!) we would have eliminated ourselves from the future.

Having distinguished ourselves in the field of arms, the only thing that was offered to us at that time, we could vigorously plant our boots on the soil of the Reich, ready to participate very actively in the edification of the future. Hitler, a soldier, was sympathetic to the courage of the soldier. A number of leaders of occupied countries were somewhat jealous of me because Hitler showed me, very ostensibly, an almost paternal affection. The statement that he made in 1944 while giving me the oak leaf Knight's Cross of the Iron Cross:[52] 'If I had a son I would like him to be like you', has been repeated everywhere. But, instead of wasting away in the political inactivity of their countries, these leaders — nobody prevented them — could, just like me, have gone and won on the Eastern Front the rights and the respect that years of combat, two dozen decorations won with difficulty and a long list of wounds inscribed on one's skin and on one's military notebooks ensured.

In any case, the Europe of soldiers had been created. It was it that would have dominated the continent with its strength, which would have unified it with its solidarity, which would have modelled it according to its ideal. The volunteers of the Eastern Front were, as one knows, half a million.

All had come to the Russian Front stuffed with suspicions and complexes. The Germans had invaded our countries. We therefore had no reason to cherish them. Some of them, in Berlin and in the occupied countries, exasperated us with their pride as dominators.

---

52 The Knight's Cross of the Iron Cross was decorated with oak leaves and, at higher levels, with swords and diamonds.

The Europe that we wanted would not be made, as they claimed, by sticking their fingers to the sides of their trousers in front of a General-Oberst or a Gauleiter.⁵³ It would be made in *equality*, without an omnipresent state imposing a lowly sergeant discipline on foreigners of second-class status.

Either equal Europeans or no Europe! Even in the middle of the war, even when we risked our skin every hour on the front beside the Germans and — the latter lacked men, of course! — *in the place of the Germans*, some agents of the SD, the famous Sicherheits Dienst, did not hesitate to report on us during full combat! I discovered many of them. I unmasked them before the troop, demanded of the German authorities official explanations, sent them to the war council, taking upon myself the functions of accuser. I obtained their condemnation to several years of imprisonment in a fortress.

In the gigantic administrative machinery of the Third Reich, false dogs and informers were not lacking. Even while hypocritically heaping flattery on us, important Germans in Brussels, not finding us malleable to their will, bombarded Berlin with 'secret' reports aiming at finding fault with us. I watched their game from close quarters. They had gone so far as to have my family correspondence from the front photocopied, in seven copies!

When I returned to Belgium, decorated with the Knight's Cross, after the breaking of the encirclement of Cherkassy, all the German 'big shots' of Brussels, who had seen the photos of Hitler receiving me with an undeniable affection, and who had sensed the truth, turned up at my property at the Drève de Lorraine to greet me there. The chief of the SD was among the lot, a colonel called Canaris — like the admiral, the leader and traitor of German counter-espionage, who ended his career in April 1945 in a rather elevated situation, which he had however not foreseen — suspended from a meat hook. When, in his turn, my Brussels Canaris approached me unctuously I asked in a stentorian voice pointing out to the audience the SD letters embroidered on his sleeve: 'Colonel, do you know what these letters signify ?'

---

53 A General-Oberst was a Colonel General and a Gauleiter was the leader of a Gau, or district, under National Socialist rule.

He had become crimson. He did not understnd. For him SD signified obviously Sicherheits Dienst. Such a question, in front of all the German generals, left him speechless. What did I really mean?

'You don't know? Oh well, I shall explain it to you, colonel: SD means Surveillance of Degrelle! The poor guy would have disappeared down the drain if he could. Everybody understood that it was better not to try any more to walk all over me, that I had hard boots. With the German conspirators these vigorous reactions were rewarding.

Neither did our temperaments correspond always. The Germans are often solemn, awkward, quite touchy. We were not delicate flowers. And a joke amused us more than stuffy words.

However, at the end of two years of common combat, common sufferings, common victories, our prejudices had fallen, friendships had been struck, political affinities had been affirmed. Youth who would have, after the war, imposed their unity of the European Front against the old reactionaries, firmly decided to remove them, generals or not, without any exaggerated ceremony, every time that their elimination would have been necessary or merely useful.

Truly, on the Eastern Front, Europe existed. Not a Europe of shopkeepers, anxious to increase, by unifying, the profit of their shop. Not a Europe of conservative military men who had, with so much intolerance, ruled their western fiefs under the occupation. But a Europe of soldiers, a Europe of idealists who, welded by the test borne in common, had finally arrived at forming from now on only a single youth, at possessing only a single political faith, at having from now on only the same conception of the future.

Comrades in the Europe of young victorious soldiers, we would have been, as on the front, equals and united, emptying overboard the omnipotent old men, bundled in the corset of their outmoded past.

The Waffen SS, described so many times, so stupidly and so unjustly, it was this: *the aristocrats of Heroism*, imposing themselves everywhere because they were the bravest, most audacious, those who had an ideal, tested through iron and fire, and who strove to make it triumph.

People have made of them the quartermasters of concentration camps. The soldier of the Waffen SS, devoted to his warlike combat, two or three thousand kilometres from his country, did not know a thing about the concenration camps. The letters of our families took sometimes a month to arrive. The arrival of a newspaper was an event. The combatant did not have the least idea of what the Jews were doing or what was being done to them in Europe at that time. When we left for Russia, not a single Jew, to our knowledge, had, as a Jew, yet been arrested in a single country of the west. The Hebrew bigwigs had all the time to get away, and did not fail to do so.

The Waffen SS did not know anything, at the front, of the fate of the Jews after 1942, who renewed ancient tragedies: for, St. Louis, who chased them from France, Isabel the Catholic, who chased them from Spain, were not Hitlerians, as far as I know.

The Waffen SS resembled a formidable cohort, like Rome and like the Napoleonic empire never knew, the most remarkable of soldiers, not only of Germany but of the whole of Europe. The non-Germans fraternised in complete equality with the Germans. This was even sometimes abnormal. We were almost better treaed than our comrades of the Reich! Few Germans were the object of the affection and consideration of Hitler as I was, a foreign leader of a division of the foreign Waffen SS.

Then, why would we have been afraid of the future, seeing the European unity that we formed, a million young men from twenty eight different countries, the most intrepid, the hardest and the best armed of all of Europe? Who would have dared to defy us? and resist ue? The future was no longer for intriguing old men, destined for future old-age homes, it was for us, the young wolves.

I knew Hitler thoroughly.

I did not fear any longer the risk of forming a team, in a common Europe, with a genius who had politically surpassed the stages of regions and nations.

'After the war', he told me, 'I will change the name of Berlin so that it will no longer appear like the capital of the Germans alone, but the capital of all'. He could create, forge, unite.

At this creation, certainly risky — but at the front we knew other risks! — exalting, at the height of the greatest dreams, how would we have preferred a return to a sordid concubinage with petty bourgeois governments, without great vices, without great virtues, under which disunited Europe would have been able, at most, to continue to flounder, as before the war, in the softest mediocrity? . . . With Hitler we took great risks. But, also, we risked great things.

It was at the moment when we had banished the greatest doubts and prepared the highest designs that adversity struck down upon us, just as an enormous rampart collapses, on the day that, under the white and icy skies of the Volga, the sinister crackling of the capitulation of Paulus at Stalingrad resounded.

Chapter X
From Stalingrad to San Sebastian

What does one think of Paulus, the German marshal, who, going down at Stalingrad at the end of January 1943, brought down in his sinking Hitler and the Third Reich? It was the misfortune, or more exactly, the error of Hitler — for it was he who had appointed him — for having had as a leader of the Sixth Army, at the crucial spot of the Russian Front and at the moment when the war was being played out, a man who had none of the indispensable qualities to receive such a shock, or, at least, to mitigate the disaster.

This disaster was total, miltarily and psychologically. One could not be more completely defeated than Paulus was. And his defeat could not have had a wider repercussion in world opinion. However, 300,000 men lost, that was not the end of the world: the Russians had lost twenty times more in a year and a half. Immense spaces remained to Hitler in the USSR and in East Germany, where he could manœuvre, and he manoeuvred until the end of April 1945.

Germany still possessed, in 1943, imposing material resources and extraordinary industrial possibilities over the entire surface of occupied Europe. At that time, Dniepropetrovsk, some thousands of kilometres from the Ruhr, still shone, in the night, with the dazzling fires of the munition factories of the Wehrmacht. And, protected by their aerial curtains of planes, the Estonian factories of Hitler continued to extract from the shale the richest petrol of the Luftwaffe.

However, Stalingrad marked the fall. There the cord was broken. One might have believed in a broken cord that could have been repaired. But the rupture was irremediable, followed by an increasingly accelerated tumble towards the abyss.

Hitler, by appointing Paulus at the head of the Sixth Corps, had not imagined that the punctilious, indecisive, military functionary that he dispatched on a major command in the Ukraine would be precisely the one who, of all his army corps chiefs, would have to assume, strategically, the greatest responsibilities. His army corps had, during the offensive of summer 1942, received a zone without special risks.

To advance towards the Caucasus, confront, more than thousand kilometres from the point of departure, the mountains, the passes, the rumbling waters which barred the access of petrols, was more risky than to make troops, perfectly seasoned, advance for some hundreds of kilometres between the Dnieper and the Don, through hardly undulating plains, until they reached a very broad river, the Volga, which could form, also, the most formidable natural line of defence of the entire Russian Front. However, it was there that everything ran aground and everything gave way.

Any other German military leader, of the Wehrmacht or the Waffen SS — a Guderian, a Rommel, a Manstein, a von Kleist, a Sepp Dietrich, a Steiner or a Gille — would have reached Stalingrad in a few weeks and would have entrenched himself there. Paulus was a senior officer of the general staff, competent when he was in his office before his map, one who made plans in rooms, a meticulous collector of statistics. These people are necessary, but within their specialisation.

By contrast, he had no idea of the real manipulation of a large unit. The highest direct command that he had exercised had been that of a batallion, that is to say, of a thousand men! And that was ten years previously! This command, very limited, had, besides, earned for him from his leader, General Heim, the following judgement: 'lack of deciding power'. Now, Hitler was going to suddenly entrust him with three hundred thousand men!

Almost all his life, Paulus had passed within the bureaucracy of the general staffs. But he was ambitious. His wife, a Romanian, rather comically nicknamed Coca, effervescent like the drink of the same name, was still more ambitious than he. She had an rritating self-importance and boastfulness. If one listened to her, she proclaimed that she was of the highest Balkan nobility, of royal blood. In fact, she bore the the commoner's, and hardly poetic, name Solescu and her father, a funny man, had left her mother a long time ago. She minced her way through all the salons. Through her indiscreet requests she belittled everything that counted in the general staff, determined to see her husband take up, quite simply, the succession to Marshal Keitel!

Hitler confided above all in faces that he knew. He saw, at every turn, the severe head of Paulus bent on his files as head of operations. He had just proceeded with numerous and sudden reorganisations at the Russian front, removing the most brilliant of the leaders whose success he had followed during the summer in order to raise generals who were too old and without a cutting edge.

He had to replace, besides, suddenly, the chief of the Sixth Corps, Marshal von Reichenau, struck by apoplexy in the snows of the Donets at 40^0 below zero. Caught unawares, Hitler designated General Paulus, whom he had under his control in his offices. The man was absolutely lamentable. When he had to undertake the offensive towards the Volga in July 1943, he should have hurried, run as all of us ran. He dallied, dragged things out, tying himself in difficulties of details, cancelling decisions that he had just taken, haunted besides by truly ridiculous personal problems of which the most marked were the deficient state of his digestive system during the entire campaign!

It is painful to see that the leader of a big unit in combat could be literally absorbed, in the midst of action, by stories that were wretched to such a degree! All of us had diarrhoea without making such a fuss! Good God, we threw ourselves on rare drinks of the steppes! Three minutes later, we left singing, relieved, our pant-buckle tightened one notch! But Paulus inundated his mail with his intestinal incontinences! Hundreds of thousands of soldiers who had drunk an excessively greasy chicken broth or rotten water did not for that reason call on the heavens and gods for help!

The mail sent post-haste by Paulus still exists. It overflows with desolate descriptions of his diarrhoeas, of old stories of sinusitis and lamentations on the material difficulties that he encountered that every leader of an important unit encountered and that were not in his body more dramatic than elsewhere! On the contrary, he had the easiest part. His march was the least long, the one where the obstacles were most reduced and, in any case, the simplest to reduce. Once the objective was attained, the Volga offered to it its enormous barrier of water ten kilometres broad and a dozen metres deep.

Instead of that, lost in the details, gnawed by apprehensions and by his ailments caused by tripe, Paulus delayed his action, leaving the enemy the time to regroup even before the crossing of the last big bend of the Don. The river was crossed, but with a delay of two weeks. Nothing seriously prevented one from launching the last attack. Those who went ahead arrived at the shore of the Volga itself.

Two or three days of vigorous exploitation of this breakthrough and Paulus, from atop the cliffs of the right bank, would not have had anything more in front of him than an empty river and, at his back, the mass of the last encircled Soviet troops. The Soviet marshal Eremenko did not live any longer cornered, suffocated, in his last eight hundred metre hole, the last in the Volga.

There too Paulus completely lacked drive, let himself be blocked these few hundred metres from final victory, foundering in limited, murderous, disappointing operations as if he had recalled only some land combats within a square metre in front of Verdun in 1917.

Everything had to work badly for this functionary who was not equal to his role. The sector that covered, in the north, the Stalingrad front had been imprudently confided, in its entirety, to Romanian and Italian contingents which had sunk themselves from the very first day of the offensive of November 1942, an offensive that the Russians had prepared in great secrecy in their bridgehead of Kremenskaya. However, the German intelligence had detected their preparations, and arrangements had been made immediately to reinforce the threatened sector. But it was destined that not a single stroke of bad luck would be spared to this unlucky Paulus.

The tanks of the twenty second German armored division which was in reserve had received from Hitler, on 10 November 1942, that is to say, nine days before the attack of the Soviets, the order to join the sector, considered to be in danger, of the Romanian Third Army. These tanks at rest had been camouflaged for a month under haystacks. Under these shelters rats — yes, rats ! — had gnawed, eaten, quite evidently, hundreds of metres of wires and cables of electrical equipment!

At the moment that they were drawn out of their shelters and set in motion, thirty nine of these hundred and four tanks could not even start: thirty seven others had to be abandoned on the way. Finally, there were no more than twenty, after nine days of technical complications, to be able to encounter the Russian offensive which, in the meanwhile, had broken the front of the Romanians some thirty hours previously and broke out like a hurricane.

Wars are like that. They are lost because of a ridiculous, or clownish, incident. A troop of bulimic rats was at the bottom of the great debacle of the Eastern Front! Without them, the hundred and four tanks of the twenty second armored division would have been able to raise their flood barrier before the Soviet assault had been unleashed. These dirty little rodent teeth had cut the nerves of the tanks. The Soviet rush found a barrier before it only thirty hours after it had broken out. Twenty tanks in all! That had escaped the appetite of the snooping snouts! More than seventy five thousand Romanian soldieres had been annihilated in the meanwhile!

However, the Don formed, west of Paulus' sector, a second barrier. Another incredible stroke of bad luck: when some Soviet tanks, ploughing through everything towards this river, appeared close to a principal bridge at Kalach, the German defenders took them for allies. The bridge was not dynamited. In five minutes, the Don was crossed!

Then Paulus lost his head. He even rushed to a plane to seek refuge in an aid post, at Nizhne Chirskaya, west of the Don, and wasted there decisive hours, isolated from his general staff, had to return, on Hitler's telephonic order, hesitated, and then more enervated than ever, not knowing what to decide. He let the columns of Soviet tanks join behind his back descending from the north and rising from the south, without having been able to imagine an intelligent march.

Nothing was still lost, for all that. Hitler had immediately launched a support tank column towards Stalingrad under the command of General Hoth, a deputy of Marshal von Manstein. It has been written a hundred times that the Führer had abandoned Paulus. Nothing is further from the truth. His tank forces arrived as far as the Mishkova river, forty eight kilometres south-west of Stalingrad, so close to Paulus that already the radios of the encircled and their liberators had established contact. The batch of messages exchanged between Paulus and Marshal von Manstein has been conserved. Reading it is saddening. Paulus could have, in forty eight hours, saved his men. It was necessary to throw himself, as well as he could, towards his liberators, with what he had at his reach and with the hundred tanks that remained to him.

One year later, caught exactly like him, with eleven divisions, in the encirclement of Cherkasy, we put up first on the terrain twenty three days of stubborn fight and then, when the tanks of General Hube that came to our support were signalled at twenty kilometres, we rushed towards them forcing a break. We lost eight thousand men during a horrible hand to hand combat, but forty five thousand passed through the breach and were saved.

Even if Paulus had lost twice as many or five times, it would have been better than to deliver his army, as he did, to death in the horror of the final encirclement or to the capitulation, which was still worse since the Soviets caused two hundred thousand prisoners of the Sixth Corps to perish, later, of misery and hunger, more than hundred and ninety thousand in their camps. Of all the prisoners of Stalingrad, nine thousand alone reappeared in their fatherland a number of years after the war.

Everything thus was better than to remain in the trap. One had to break out. Paulus did not manage to make any decision. Von Manstein called him again by radio; he sent, by plane, officers of his general staff into the core of Stalingrad itself, in order to make him start finally.

His tank columns, under the command of Hoth, had advanced as a spearhead, they increasingly ran the risk of being encircled in their turn if the tergiversations of Paulus were going to be prolonged. It was then that the latter, shaken by his mania, carped about meticulous regroupments on a bureaucratic basis and who, in fact, preferred deep down not to move any more, telegraphed to his liberators that he would need six days to finalise his preparations for extrication!

Six days! In six days, in 1940, Guderian and Rommel had moved from the Meuse to the North Sea! Paulus and his Sixth Corp did not escape the disaster of Stalingrad because the leader did not have either strength of will or a decisive mind. Salvation was under his nose, forty eight kilometres away.

The unheard of effort of the liberation tanks, that had arrived very close to him and which he could have joined in two days, was in vain. Paulus, an incompetent theoretician on land, a soft mind, melted even before making a decision, just let the liberating column exhaust itself waiting for him. He did not appear at all. He did not even try to appear. Von Manstein's tanks, after an interminable and extremely dangerous wait, had to break out and return to their base.

Paulus finished a month later even more miserably. He should have, at least, had himself killed at the head of his last troops. He stretched out on his bed in his underground command post, waited for negotiators of his general staff to finish long discussions with some Soviet emissaries outside. He asked, with a painful insistence, that once he had surrendered, a car be placed at his disposal to drive him to the general headquarters of the enemy. His soldiers were in agony. He was thinking of a car to transport him. The man is fully revealed here.

Some hours later, received at dinner by the Russian command, he asked for some vodka and raised his glass, before the stunned Soviet generals, in honour of the Red Army which had just defeated him! The text of this little speech still exists, recorded immediately, as one may imagine, by the Intelligence Services of the Soviets. This text is nauseating. Two hundred thousand soldiers of Paulus had died or left for camps where an atrocious death awaited them. He, vodka in hand, saluted the victorious Communists!

He was taken to Moscow by a special train, in a sleeping-car. Already this military man who was ever indecisive was no more, politically and morally, than a wreck. He was, already then, ripe for betrayal. He escaped the gallows of Nuremberg for that reason. He would return to install himself in East Germany. There he vegetated for some years more. He died a long time ago. But this mediocre military man, pusillanimous and lacking in will, had broken the back of his country's army.

Like a cat with a broken back, the Wehrmacht stretched itself out two years more on the routes of defeat, tenacious and heroic. But it had lost the day when Paulus, refusing to take a risk, had destroyed, before the whole world, the myth of the invincibility of the Third Reich.

The proof that Paulus could have resisted and free himself and even win his battle was administered, that winter itself, by Marshal von Manstein, that Paulus had not dared to come when he could have — and should have — thrown all his encircled troops vigorously towards their liberators.

The latter lashed out for three months against the Russians, who, freed from the army of Paulus behind them, had been able to run forward hundreds of kilometres, going beyond the Don, the Donets, submerging a part of the Ukraine. When they had hurtled towards the west, Manstein cornered them once again, beat them soundly, reconquered Kharkov with flying colours, partially and temporarily neutralising the disaster of the Volga.

If Paulus had thrown himself towards Manstein, fighting later beside him, or if he had held on tight to the ruins of Stalingrad upto the middle of spring — this was not strictly unfeasible — the war would, perhaps, have still been won, or, at least, the Soviets would have been contained for a longer time.

In spite of everything that was atrocious about the fight for Stalingrad, possibilities of resistance remained. Considerable stocks of ammunition and food supplies were captured by the Russians in the conquered Stalingrad. The aerial bridge had given a support which had not been total, but which had nevertheless been quite considerable. Just the twenty three thousand encircled horses and beasts of burden at the same time as the troops represented millions of kilos of utilisable meat. The statistics of the reserves provided by Paulus were false, as all statistics provided by fighting units are false that reveal half of what they possess and ask for double of what they need. In Leningrad, with *thirty times less* food, the Russians resisted for two years and won, finally.

And then, in any case, to prolong, even in the worst sufferings, the resistance in Stalingrad, was better than to send two hundred thousand survivors to die of suffering in the famine camps of the Soviets.

Tank divisions were brought in haste from France to free the besieged. Every month that was won counted. In the meanwhile, new arms could have been used, capable of changing everything. Jet fighters, variable geometry aircraft, were invented in the Reich already, whereas the Allies had no idea of these. The German rockets too were going to be operational in 1944, if luck had not put Hitler at a disadvantage, notably when his heavy water factory in Norway was bombed, an atomic bomb like that of Hiroshima would have fallen before 1945 on Moscow, or on London, or on Washington as well. On another level, it was not unimaginable that Churchill and Roosevelt realised, before it was too late, that they were in the process of delivering half the world to the USSR.

They could have, in time, given up placing at Stalin's disposal the four hundred and fifty thousand lorries, the thousands of aircraft and tanks, the fabulous raw materials and the war materials that assured the Soviets their domination from the Kuril islands to the Elba. It would therefore have been better to hold on, hold on on the bank of the Volga, at the Dnieper, at the Vistula, at the Oder. Every campaign used to bar the way to the Red armies would have perhaps saved the millions of free men of Europe threatened by death.

After Stalingrad, once the possibilities of military resistance of the Third Reich had been reaffirmed and once Kharkov had been conquered, the hope survived for some months more of retaking the initiative for a third time.

After the first winter, the restarting of the European armies had demanded an enormous effort, for Stalin had had the time to adapt to the lightning war, and, especially, to unlocking its secret. The race to the Caucasus had been realised, but, to tell the truth, had been lost because the major part of the enemy had slipped between our fingers. After a second winter and after the disaster of Stalingrad, morally much more important than militarily, a third offensive would become still more difficult, so much more now that, in the meantime, everything had changed in the west.

The Allies had disembarked in North Africa, had spread all along the Suez Canal. Rommel had lost the country and was no longer the old Roman proconsul but a bitter, sour creature, the latest victim of intrigues. The European continent could have been invaded at any time, and it was that very year which saw the Yankees chewing their chewing gum under the orange trees of Palermo and run after girls on the dark alleys of Naples that smelt of jasmine and urine.

The last attempt was risked anyway. The powerful mass of all the Panzer Divisons which remained available was launched anew towards Kursk, near Orel, in July 1943, for a big battle of annihilation of the Soviet materials, which, if it had succeeded, would have delivered to us finally, after so many assaults, the big rivers and the large plains upto Asia.

The test was decisive. The Soviets had had good training. Their German masters from 1941 and 1942 had taught them everything.

Their factories, set up in the shelter of the Ural mountains, had fabricated for them thousands upon thousands of tanks. The Americans had stupidly done the rest, freely gifting them with raw materials in gigantic quantities and the most modern armaments. Behind us the Anglo-American airforce ground everything down to facilitate to the Soviets the path towards the European prey.

The Kursk-Orel duel was hallucinating. Hitler had engaged on this narrow terrain as many tanks and planes as on the entire stretch of the Russian Front during the general assault of June 1941. For several days, thousands of German and Soviet tanks fought iron against iron. But the original double breach of the armies of the Reich shrank from day to day, was stopped and neutralised. The German army, this time, was really defeated. It could not have passed through.

The proof had just been given that the Russian resources had become stronger. It was there that the Second World War was lost, at Kursk and near Orel, and not at Stalingrad, for three hundred thousand men lost, accidentally, out of eleven million combatants did not mean an irremediable disaster. The irremediable disaster was this decisive duel of the tank armies of Hitler and Stalin, on the Kursk-Orel battlefied at the very centre of Russia, in July 1943.

From that time, the immense Russian streamroller had only to descend towards the civilised countries of the west. The only thing that one could still do was to prevent it from descending too fast, with the hope of stopping it somehow before it reached the heart of Europe.

To save what could be saved we fought still, for all of two years, two terrible years, when one lost in one week more men than before in a trimester. We hung on to the terrain, we let ourselves be encircled in order to retain the enemy for ten days, twenty days at most. We escaped only at the cost of apocalyptic sorties and breaches, leaving behind us, in the nocturnal snows, the continuing desperate cries of the dying: 'Comrades, comrades . . . ' Poor comrades that the snows covered slowly, those snows which more than once had been our only food . . . It was necessary to rush through Russian villages on fire, among the wounded who writhed with pain on the reddened ice, among the horses which struggled, disembowelled, their entrails expanded like frightful brown and green serpents. The last tanks threw themselves towards the sacrifice or, more precisely, towards extermination. Entire units were massacred on the spot.

But the fronts were pierced everywhere, were gaping wide. Dozens of thousands of tanks, millions of Mongols and Circassians, extended towards Poland, Romania, Hungary, Austria, then to Silesia and eastern Prussia. We resisted without cease, reconquering German villages overcome by the Soviets some hours earlier: the old men castrated agonised on the ground in swamps of blood: the women, the very old as well as the young, raped fifty times, eighty times, lay sticky, their hands and legs still tied to stakes.

It was this martyrdom of Europe that we had wished to delay, to limit to a degree that it was still possible to do. Our boys died in thousands to contain these horrors, to permit the deserters to run behind us towards the havens of a west that was increasingly shrinking.

When one blames Hitler for having maintained fight for so long one does not take into account that, without his fanatical will, without his draconian orders of standing resistance, without the executions and the hangings of the generals who retreated and of soldiers who deserted, dozens of millions of Europeans of the east would have also been attacked, overwhelmed and would experience today the stifling servitude of the Balts, Polish, Hungarians and Czechs.

Immolating the remainder of his army in a desperate hand-to-hand combat, one soldier against hundred soldiers, one tank against hundred tanks, Hitler, whatever his responsibility had been at the beginning of the Second World War, saved millions of Europeans who, without him, without his energy, and without all our poor dead, would not have been — and for a long time — any more than slaves.

When Hitler blew his brains out, what could have been saved had been saved. The trembling columns of the last refugees had

From Stalingrad to San Sebastian

reached Bavaria, the Elba, Schleswig-Holstein. Then only the smoke of Hitler's corpse rose under the shredded trees of his garden. The arms had fallen silent. The tragedy had ended.

When the capitulation had been made public the last combatants constituted only isolated groups, often cut off from all contact with their command. The few comrades who surrounded me did not wish, any more than I did, to cede, to surrender. A plane had been abandoned in our sector, the Norwegian sector that we had reached at the end of an interminable combat along the Baltic, Estonia, Denmark. We gathered petrol from here and there. We would have to cross two thousand three hundred kilometres if we wished to reach a country like Spain that had remained outside the fray.

Did we have a chance in a thousand to come out of it? Flying more than two thousand kilometres above the enemy, his anti-aircraft artillery, his bases of fighters, we would be pelted hundred times. But we preferred everything to capitulation.

We ventured into the air in the middle of the night, crossed the whole of Europe in the daze of Allied shooting. We reached at dawn the Bay of Biscay. Our engines snorted, choked, the petrol reserves were exhausted. Were we going to perish a few minutes away from Spain? . . . We had decided, if necessary to land, no matter how; if we were not killed on the ground, we would take by force no matter what car. With the sputtering of the six machine-guns that we carried we would have anyway probably reached the frontier. But no, the plane continued to function. We could take it up a last time, pour on the two engines the last decilitres of petrol that remained at the end of reserves. We flew back into the void. We did not have the time to see anything. We grazed pink roofs, we steered towards a clear bay. Then an enormous rock rose before our eyes. Too late! We stepped on the brakes, at three hundred kilometres an hour, with just the outer shell of the mechanism. An engine exploded in the air. Already the plane had bifurcated, crazed, it ran into the waves, and crashed there.

In front of us, at the end of the shining waters, San Sebastian was waking up. From the top of the embankment two *guardias civiles* shook the black fan of waxed cloth of their cap. The water had invaded the broken plane upto twenty centimetres away from the roof, just enough to let us breathe still.

We were all a mess, with broken bones, torn flesh. But nobody was dead, nor even dying. Some light boats approached, collected us, reached the beach. An ambulance took me. I spent fifteen months, very wounded, at the Mola military hospital. My political life was over. My soldier's life was over. The most thankless of all, that of a hunted, hated exile had begun.

Chapter XI
The Exiled

'My dear Degrelle . . . ' It's Himmler addressing me. We were entrenched, in the middle of the night of 2 May 1945 in the mud of a dark camp. Five metres in front of us a thousand Allied planes had just destroyed the city of Kiel. Everything rose in clear bunches like fused metal, rendering darker the night in which we were huddled. 'My dear Degrelle, you should survive. Everything will change quickly. You should get yourself six months. Six months . . .'

He fixed me with his little ferret's eyes, behind his glasses which shone with every spray of the explosions. His round face, normally of a moon-like pallour, had become pallid in these end-of-the-world collapses.

Some hours earlier, at the end of the afternoon, we had lost Lübeck. Pinned down by the English tanks and machine-gunned by the Tipfligers, we had surged back on the Denmark highway when I saw Himmler hurtling down a country lane in a big black car. Already, a short while previously, I had bumped into Speer, the former minister of armaments, architect extraordinary and the gentlest man in the world. He, in this deluge of fire, remained, as always, naturally cheerful. We had joked together for an instant. Himmler had come in. He did not joke often. In any case, when he did, it was always studiously. In this twilight of 2 May 1945 — Hitler was dead fifty hours and had left him out of any succession — Himmler had a more austere face than ever, colourless, shining under four thin meagre hairs. He had tried to smile at me, between his teeth, which were small, a rodent's teeth under which, already, was hidden the little pod of potassium cyanide which would strike him down a few days later.

I had climbed into the car next to him. We had made a stop in a farmyard. He had announced to me that I had become a general a few days earlier. General, corporal, that hardly mattered any more! The world fell down upon us. Soon we would all be without uniforms and without epaulettes. And even dead, for the most part.

We had together taken again, in the night, the route to the big port of Kiel. When we were about to enter it, the airforce of the Allies had offered prodigious fireworks of final annihilation. All of Kiel rose into the air, was roasted. On our way the bombs tumbled down like nuts, exploded and richoteted. We had time only to jump into a marshy field. One of the two secretaries of Himmler, a tall unattractive girl, had immediately lost in the swamp her two high-heeled slip-ons. Perched on one of her calves, which were bony and skinny, she rummaged in the black mud, seeking in vain to recover her shoes and lamenting. Every person has his own preoccupations.

Himmler continued with his. 'My dear Degrelle, six months, six months . . .' I had often collided with him on account of my intransigence. An intellectually mediocre man, he would have been a strict schoolteacher, in normal times. The European views were beyond him. But, finally, he had become accustomed to my points of view and my manners. At the moment when our universe collapsed, it was important for him that I survive.

Already, on 21 April 1945, after the Oder, he had asked me to be the minister of foreign affairs of the government that would succeed Hitler's team. He had afterwards sent me General Steiner to get my assent.

I thought it was a joke. I was the last that could have dealt, as minister of foreign affairs, with the Allies, all of whom were looking out for me, to hang me as quickly as possibly! Mired in the mud, Himmler repeated tenaciously: 'Everything will have changed in six months!' Finally, I replied to him, staring, in the brilliance of the explosions, at his small tired eyes: 'Not in six months, Reichsführer, in six years!' I should have said: in sixty years! And now I think even in sixty years the chances, for me, of any political resurrection will be even smaller! The only resurrection which awaited me henceforth would be that of the Last Judgement, with loud blows of apocalyptic trumpets!

The exiled person, naturally, has a tendency to believe that his chances will return. He watches the horizon. The least symptom of modification in his lost country is invested in his eyes with a capital importance. An election, a press incident of no interest, puts him in a state of effervescence. 'Everything is going to change!' Nothing changes. The months pass, the years pass.

At the beginning the special exiled person was recognised. One watched wherever he went. Today hundred persons come into contact with him indifferently: the fat woman who bumps into him thinks of her leeks that she needs to buy; the man, too slow in front of her, ogles the passers-by; the boy who runs banging his shinbones does not have the least idea of who he is, and especially of what he was. He is only an unknown person in the heap. Life has passed on, washed over everything, the existence of the proscribed has become colourless like the rest.

In May 1945, when I found myself in a small iron bed in the hospital of Saint-Sebastian, plastered from the neck to the left foot, I was still a star. The big military governor had come in covered in big ribbons, expanding in noisy hugs! He had not yet well understood that I had fallen from the bad side and that I was no longer to be frequented. He would understand it soon! Everybody would understand it soon!

At the end of fifteen months, when my bones had been mended again, I found myself one night, quite far from there, in a black street, guided towards a secret cottage. The only solution for me, the only survival, when one asked for my extradition on all sides — twelve bullets in the skin! — was the hole of oblivion. I would spend two years in a hole of oblivion. I would know many others! I was installed in a sombre little room, beside a service life. I could not see anybody. I could never approach a window. The shutters remained always lowered.

The two old people who accommodated me constituted my entire world. He weighed hundred and fifty kilos. The first thing that I perceived in the morning was his chamber pot with urine in the corridor. He produced four litres of it in a night. Intensive work. His only work. Already before the afternoon meal he dressed in pyjamas, a gigantic pair, open, wide open, on a big triangle of pale flesh.

She trotted around under a bunch of rare yellow and thick hair, navigating in the darkness of her house — light burns! — on two old rags, worn out slippers!

In the evening they both listened, ensconced in wicker armchairs, a theatre play on the radio. At the end of five minutes they were asleep, he coughing deep grunts in front, she, her head thrown back, behind, emitting strident whistling sounds. At one in the morning the silence of the end of the broadcast woke them up. She then took up the bird cage; he a big painted statue of St. Joseph brandishing a green palm. They began to walk slowly towards their bedroom. The snoring recommenced. In the morning I found again in front of the door the four litres of urine.

Such would be my life for two years: solitude, silence, shadows, two old people who filled a pot completely, carried St. Joseph and two budgerigars. I did not see a smile a single time. Nor two attractive legs on a pavement. Not even a tree with yellowed leaves against a background of the sky.

Afterwards, I had to leave. My wound in the stomach — a gift of the Caucasus — had burst open from one end to the other. In six months, I had lost thirty two kilos. In a discreet clinic, they had opened my stomach, from the esophagus to navel, seventeen centimetres.

I had been recognised at the end of three days by a nurse. I had to be taken away on a stretcher in the middle of the night. I was lifted up on a narrow stairwy to the fourth floor. I dripped with sweat and blood, for, under the contorsions of the stretcher, all the sutures had come out! What a life! Not to show oneself — in order not to be recognised — is useless. One recognises you anyway, one

The Exiled

sees you anyway, even if you are two thousand kilometres away from there.

I possess a really comical file on my stay in twenty different countries. One day a journalist had discovered me in Lima! Another day it was in Panama! Or in the Argentine pampas! Or in a villa near the Nile, at Colonel Nasser's! Every time the details were so precise that I ended by wondering if I was not really there, if I was not mistaken.

A big French newspaper brought, under enormous front page headlines, absolutely complete details on my life in Brazil, on my way of dressing, eating, speaking. As a true Parisian reporter, the author expanded at great length, naturally, on my loves! Yes, I loved! I loved a negress! And I even had a fine little mulatto from that! Would the reader, in spite of everything, doubt it? Doubt! But the photo is there! The photo of my son, the little negro, a kid of three or four years, with round eyes, locks of curly hair stretching on his skull like a moss carpet! My mother-in-law, a pious lady of the Périgord, jumped up at breakfast reading these rather unexpected revelations in her customary daily routine! This secret grandson did not really please her at all. I had some difficulty in making her know that I had never, in my life, set foot in Brazil, that no mulatto had entered my family.

No matter. Thirty times, fifty times, I had to learn that I was in Caracas, in Valparaiso, in Cuba — where a poor devil was put in prison in my place! — and even in the hold of the ship *Monte Ayala*, inspected in the high seas by the Americans, at the end of August 1946 — thus fifteen months after the war! — and brought back to the port of Lisbon, where it was searched thoroughly for several days: an American policeman even climbed up the chimney to the top in order to see if I was not hanging on to the soot!

A secret service report described me entering a wood with a Portuguese colonel! The Intelligence Service had noticed me in Gibraltar! Other journalists had followed me to the Vatican! Others, to a port of the Atlantic, where I bought cannons! I was seen even in Anvers, where, it seems, I went to breathe the country air.

Occasionally, it is true, I was discovered by an idiot or by a follower who fell into my arms weeping. I got away by collecting my belongings and scooting elsewhere. I sometimes also met some enemies. It was always funny. They had clamoured for my head, and suddenly they were in front of me. First stupefaction. Curiosity overcame it. In short, amusing, the air was cleared.

One day I even had the surprise of finding myself seated in a little popular restaurant, beside one of the most well-known leaders of the Belgian Socialist party, a man from Liège. I had not paid enough attention to him.

He neither. He was at table with a big blond woman built like a Mercury. I was reading my newspaper. I looked up, our eyes met. He was for a second taken aback. Then he smiled, winked at me. He too would not lead me to the gallows!

The only people who hunted me, everywhere, with a truly diabolical hatred, were the Jews. The Belgian government, of course, had hunted me for a long time with hostility. It called for my extradition twenty times.

But, nevertheless, Spaak, the Minister of Foreign Affairs, did not dare to go too far. He was not self-righteous. He had done everything, in June and July 1940, to obtain from the Germans power to return to the Brussels of the Occupation. He had bombarded them with telegrams, setting in motion throughout Europe all his contacts. I was quite informed of these manœuvres.

His friend and president, the former Socialist minister de Man, had even communicated to me the letters that Spaak had written, in Brussels, to his wife, in order that he would have had from Hitler the authorisation to show up. 'Henri de Man always had a weakness for you', wrote Spaak to his wife to motivate her to find Henri, who, with a sardonic glint, burst out laughing at my table while reading these words !

Hitler did not accept Spaak's request, which was repeated ten times. That is why Spaak dashed off to London. But without the opposition of Hitler, he had fully entered the system, as de Man had entered it, already in May 1940.

The Exiled

As for the Jews, it was a completely different affair. Never had REX been really anti-Semitic, before the war. The polemical manœuvres of the Jews infuriated me, it is true. It is also true that I do not hold them dear in my heart. They get on my nerves. But I rather left them alone. At REX, they could be members of the movement like anybody else. The leader of REX Brussels, during our victory of 1936, was a Jew. Even in 1942, in the middle of the German occupation, the secretary of my successor Victor Mattys was Jewish. He was called Kahn, which says everything!

I did not know of concentration camps, crematory ovens. Nevertheless, the Jews got it into their head, after the war, that a big anti-Semitic movement had been reconstituted throughout the world and that I was its leader.

First, I was not its leader. Then, if that was regrettable or not, it did not exist. Thus there was no question of anti-Jewish persecutions or organisations.

For twenty five years the Christians have not worried too much. Nevertheless, to decapitate an absolutely non-existant organisation by liquidating me, some Jewish leaders, of the highest echelons, belonging notably to the national secuirty of the Israeli state, mounted abduction expeditions against me one after the other.

Nothing was lacking: the big black Lincoln with rear tank reconverted into a sort of narcotic coffin in which I would be transported unconscious: the boat that awaited me at the nearby coast to take me to Tel Aviv; five revolvers to knock me off if I resisted; six million to pay for the accomplices; the complete plans of my residences and their entrances. The preceding night, the telephone and electrical lines had been cut on my hill, the dogs of the neighbouring properties had been poisoned.

It was just a close shave that, in a July burning with the sun, I did not go there. The Israeli aggressors, led by a very well-known Jew, the journalist Zwi Aldouby, were caught, armed to the teeth, when they were on the point of succeeding.

They were sentenced to eight, ten and twelve years in prison. Another operation was mounted, almost simultaneously, by means of a helicopter, from a Moroccan port. Some years later, a new abduction-assassination was attempted. This time, the Jewish aggressors had arrived by sea, coming from Anvers. It was a Jewess indeed who informed one of my sisters of the plot, wishing to thank me, she said, for having saved her life during the war. At that time, I, like everybody would have done, tried to save all the people who I knew were anxious. But I did not draw up lists for the post-war period! Even if I do not even remember this Jewess that I saved then and who saved me afterwards!

Her warning came at the right time, the three members of the expedition were locked up, hardly disembarked. But it is rattling. Every time I had to move, hide in country residences of old friends, or in a brewery or, for long months, in a cell — not funny I beg you to believe — of a Benedictine cloister. I shall remember a long time the *Benedicamus Domino* shouted at five in the morning by the one who woke the others up for the service! But to move constantly also means the impossibility of earning a living, having a fixed occupation in any place, or simply having a roof over one's head, if one is always threatened and if one has to always flee elsewhere.

Journalists' interviews too did not fail to complicate my life as a proscribed person, by often, and in an untimely manner, calling attention to my name. Dozens of these interviews have been published, all invented like crime novels. Twice, a long time ago, I received in my shelters 'special envoys' who afterwards presented my statements completely falsely, when they had promised, of course, to send me the texts for initial agreement. Since then I have avoided journalists like the plague!

One is always remade by them because their objective is different: they search for something sensational, to publish quickly. But the truth is not exposed under facile headlines at such speed. Only once a magazine published a real interview with me. It wanted it. I wanted to have it believed at that time that I was in Buenos Aires in a clinic.

The text appeared in its entirety. The magazine knew perfectly that no reporter of its team had seen me, and that I was not in

The Exiled

Buenos Aires in any way. What did it matter to it? The main thing was that the public emit oh's and ah's all through their reading of it!

One explains to them what Mr. Onassis and the ex-Mrs. Kennedy do in their bed, and the state of the ovaries, with designs to support, of Queen Fabiola, when none of these editors is a manservant or a nurse! When the journalist travels, it is because he wishes to get some fresh air at the expense of the princess and draw up really stimulating travel expenses. He sniffs the air, renders homage to the beauties of the vintage, then writes up his copy very rapidly and in haste. The only thing that remains is to touch up the article.

But the exiled person, how does he see the public? He too, with the passing of time, is going to imagine only an unreal, non-existent public. He lends to it a way of thinking that it does not have, that it does not have anymore. He has lost the thread of the development. Everything changes, and he does not know that everything has changed. The world is no longer as it was, the people are no longer as he knew them. Like any old industrial worker overtaken by modern life, he has to readapt himself. He continues to believe that the methods of the past are still valid, that one is still excited about them, and about him.

Who is interested in one after some years? People are eclipsed. Events succeed one another. Each of us throws the one before us into the ditch of oblivion. The exile remains convinced that he is still on the stage of the present.

Now, the curtain has been lowered a long time ago. He waits for applause to revive as if the public was always in front of his tribunal, not taking into consideration that the years have pushed it into the wings. This quid pro quo is often painful. Who is going to say to an exile that he does not count any more? He does not realise it. Especially if he does not wish to realise it. His smile is often contracted, but it is his last way of convincing himself that the future is not closed to him definitively . . .

I too, for a long time, believed in survival. I was very young. At thirty eight I was not going to disappear in this way, ever! Oh well! but yes, one disappears! Friends die in the distance, one after the other. The past becomes fluid, like a river which thins down and then finally disappears from the view of navigators. For a boy of twenty years, who was not born when we had collapsed, who are we? . . . He mixes everything up. Or he does not even know anything more of our stories, which do not excite him any more than the red moustaches of Vercingetorix or the decayed teeth of Louis XIV.

That's not all: there is a stampede in the trade. The exiles succeed one another, they pile up on one another. Already the Perons, the Trujillos,[54] the Batistas,[55] the Abbés Fulbert Youlou,[56] defeated much after us, are only silhouettes now, hardly detectable. The names of Lagaillarde,[57] Ortiz[58] and even Bidault[59] and Soustelle,[60] the two last political stars of the Algerian affair, no longer mean anything, after five years, to 90% of the French. We are in the century of speed. Disappearing from the visual field of the public is also speedy.

Even for very informed people, a political figure exiled for twenty five years has become an almost unreal being. They think he has disappeared. Or they do not think that he is still alive. One evening I was invited to dine at a medical conference, known

---

54 Rafael Trujillo (1891–1961) was a Dominican dictator who was assassinated in 1961.
55 Fulgencio Batista (1901–1973) was Cuban president from 1940 to 1944 and US-backed dictator from 1952 to 1959, when he was overthrown by Castro's Cuban Revolution.
56 Abbé Fulbert Youlou (1917–1972) was an anti-Communist Roman Catholic priest who became the first president of the Republic of the Congo in 1960. He was brought down by a revolution in 1963.
57 Pierre Lagaillarde (1931–2014) was a French Algerian and anti-Independence activist during the Algerian War of 1954 to 1962.
58 Joseph Ortiz (1917–1995) was a partisan of the French Algeria movement during the Algerian War.and founder of the OAS (Organisation de l'armée secrète) militia in Algeria.
59 Georges Bidault (1899–1983) was a French politician who participated in the French Resistance during the Second World War but, opposed to de Gaulle's policy of Algerian independence, collaborated with the Algerian OAS.
60 Jacques Soustelle (1912–1990) was a French anthropologist who served as Governor General of Algeria. He opposed Algerian independence and joined the OAS.

internationally, and very close to the head of state of the country where I resided at that time. Some very famous persons entered. Each of these invitees had known me at diverse stages of my exile, and under different names. For some I had been Enrique Duran, Polish (with a funny Polish name!). For others Lucien Demeure, Frenchman. For others yet Juan Sanchez. For others Pepe, nothing more. I was tired of deploying, at every handshake, this panoply of false names.

When a big banker whom I had never met entered, I did not hesitate to introduce myself under my real name: Léon Degrelle! He looked at me amused. 'And I am Benito Mussolini.' I sweated to convince him that I was indeed who I was and that I had not been joking!

In this way, with the passing of time, the exile slips into obscurity or into oblivion. He has moved from the Mercedes of power to the ill-smelling metro of exile. It takes time for the most lucid to come to terms with that. The exile prefers to hang on. He believed in something that was, at one moment of his life, exceptional. He suffers horribly from being transferred from this exceptional thing to the ordinary, to the common restaurant with cheap prices, with four penny linen. The big dream dislocated, disintegrated, disturbs him. He begins often to believe again that, nevertheless, one never knows, something could resurge. Something, yes. But we, no. We are finished.

It is better to come to terms in a manly manner and to draw up the balance. The fascisms have had an impact on their time, and on the future beyond their time. That is what counts. What have they left behind? What have they changed?

Independently of our personal lives, so loud with dynamism yesterday, eliminated now, the true problem that is posed is this: of this great adventure — or epic — of fascisms, once the tombs are closed, what remains of them? what will remain of them?

Chapter XII
And if Hitler had won?

That is the big question.

If Hitler had won?

Let us assume that, since it was for a long time possible that such an event might occur. In Ocotber 1941, Hitler was very close to conquering Moscow (he reached its suburbs) and to crossing the river Volga from its source (he had reached it) to its mouth (it was within his reach). Moscow waited only for the appearance of the tanks of the Reich on the Kremlin Square to revolt. Stalin would have fled.

It would have been the end. Some German colums of occupation, like those of Admiral Kolchak[61] in 1919, would have promptly crossed Siberia or would have parachuted there. Close to the Pacific Ocean the swastika would have flown at Vladivostok, ten thousand kilometres from the Rhine.

What would have been the reactions in the world? England of the end of 1941 could have laid down its arms at anytime. It would have sufficed that on one evening of excessive whisky Churchill collapsed into an armchair, drooling, struck by apoplexy. That this inveterate drunkard had maintained himself so long on alcohol is a case for doctors. His personal doctor besides published, after his death, some very comical details of the Bacchic resistance of his illustrious patient.

---

[61] Alexander Kolchak (1874–1920) was an Imperial Russian admiral who established an anti-Communist government in Siberia that was supported by the Whites. He was betrayed by the Czechoslovak Legion and executed by the Bolsheviks.

And if Hitler Had Won?

But, even alive, Churchill depended on the mood of his public. The English public tried still, in 1941, to cope. But it was tired. The conquest of Russia by Hitler, using the entire Luftwaffe, would have completely crushed it. This war, what was it leading to? To what, besides, had it led? England finished the war fully denuded, deprived of the entirety of its empire and relegated, internationally, to the rank of a secondary nation, at the end of its five year strip-tease. A Chamberlain in the place of Churchill would have, a long time ago, attached a white flag to the tip of his umbrella.

In any case, just faced with a victorious Germany — displaying an empire without equal in the world and filled with everything, over ten thousand kilometres wide, from the Anglo-Norman islands of the North Sea to the Sakhalin islands in the Pacific — England could not have been more than a raft burst by a tornado. It could no longer have resisted for a long time on the waves. Churchill — and the English before him — would have tired himself emptying with buckets the water of an increasingly flooded hull. Find refuge abroad? In Canada? Churchill, bottle by his side, would have become there a trapper or a small café owner, but not a saviour. In Africa? In India? The British Empire was already lost. It could not be the last springboard of a resistance that no longer had any sense.

One would not even have spoken any more of de Gaulle, who would have become a professor in Ottawa, rereading Saint-Simon in the evening or holding in his hands the tangle of knitting wool of the hardworking Aunt Yvonne.[62]

The English victory was really the stroke of luck of a stubborn old man functioning on alcohol, holding on to a cracked mast with sinister crackles, and for whom the gods of drunkards had an exceptional indulgence.

No matter! Once the USSR was in the hands of Hitler, in the autumn of 1941, the English resistance would have lasted for a long time, without Churchill or with Churchill. As for the Americans, they had not yet entered the war at that time. Japan was watching out for them, prepared to jump on their backs. Hitler, once Europe

---

62 Yvonne de Gaulle (1900–1979) was the wife of Charles de Gaulle and nicknamed 'tante Yvonne'.

was his, would not have had to involve himself in Japan any more than Japan, in June 1941, had involved itself in the German offensive in the USSR.

The United States, occupied in Asia for a long time, would not have added one more war on their back in Europe. The United States-Hitler military conflict would not have taken place — in spite of the belligerent itches of the old Roosevelt, blanched, cadaverous in his hackney coachman's cape, in spite of the excitations of his wife Eleanor, all teeth bulging, teeth bulging like a donkey's, similar to the sprockets of a caterpillar wheel.

Let us assume thus that at the end of autumn 1941 — he would have been there in a quarter of an hour by tram — Hitler would have been installed in the Kremlin, as he had been installed in Vienna in 1937, in Prague in 1939, and in the armistice wagon in Compiègne in 1940.

Quid ? What would have happened in Europe?

Hitler would have unified Europe with force, that is beyond doubt.

Everthing great that is done in the world is done through force. It is regrettable, one would say. It would certainly be more decent that the good people, the patronesses of the parishes and the fearless vestals of the Salvation Army, would gather us in a democratic manner in peaceful territorial units, smelling of chocolate, mimosa and holy water. But never did it happen that way.

The Capets did not raise the Kingdom of France through universal suffrage elections. Apart from one or other province shed in the royal bed, at the same time as his night-dress, by a wriggling young wife, the remainder of the French territory arose through guns or bombarding. In the north, conquered by the royal armies, the inhabitants were chased out of their towns — Arras notably — like rats. In the south, in the Albigeois that resisted Louis VIII, the Cathars, beaten, whipped, thrashed by the royal Crusaders, were roasted in their fortified castles, a sort of crematory ovens before Hitlerism. The Protestants of Coligny found themselves at the end of the pikes of St. Bartholomew, or hung from the cords of the gallows of Montfaucon. The Revolution of the Marats and the Fouquier-Tinvilles preferred, in order to establish its authority, the shining steel of the guillotine and its basket of barn, to drafts of coarse red wine for the voters at the corner café.

Even Napoleon skewered with the bayonet each of the borders of his empire. Catholic Spain did not invite the Moors to become Spanish at the rhythm of its castanets. It disembowelled them vigorously during seven centuries of the Reconquista, until the last of the Abencerrages ran for his life and found again the palms and coconut trees of the shores of Africa. The Arabs had not thought of unifying in a more amiable way, to their advantage, the south of Spain, they who nailed the resisting Spaniards to the doors of the cities such as Cordoba, between a dog and a pig crucified on either side and vociferating indignantly.

In the last century, Bismarck forged the German unity with the cannon, at Sadowa and Sedan. Garibaldi did not gather together the Italian lands with the rosary in his hand but by taking Pontifical Rome by storm. The states of America themselves became United only after the extermination of the old owners, the Red Skins, and after four years of hardly democratic killings during the war of Secession. And still! Twenty million Blacks live, at this hour, against their will, under the stick of millions of Whites who, in the last century, continued to tatoo their fathers and mothers with red iron, exactly as if they had been colts or mules. As regards inscription on their electoral lists, it was very basic. They did not even vote besides, once the branding was over!

Only the Swiss constituted, more or less peacefully, their little state with cafe-owners, crossbowmen, milkmaids and milkmen. But, apart from the gleam of William Tell's apple, their worthy cantons hardly shone in the history of international politics. The great empires, the great states, were all constituted by force. That's regrettable? That's a fact.

Hitler, camping in a recalcitrant Europe would certainly not have done other than Caesar commandeering the Gauls, than Louis XIV taking over Artois and Roussillon, than the English conquering the

Irish, pillaging them, persecuting them, than the Americans turning the cannons of their cruisers on the Philippines, on Puerto Rico, on Cuba, on Panama, and taking, with rocket attacks, their military frontiers upto the 37th Parallel in Vietnam. Democracy, that is to say, the electoral consent of the peoples, comes only afterwards, when everything is over.

The masses see the universe through the key-hole of the lock of their little personal preoccupations. Never would a Breton, a Flemish man, a Catalan of Roussillon, have of their own accord opened up to integrate themselves into a French unity. The man from Baden wished to remain that *mordicus*.[63]

The man from Württemberg a man from Württemberg. The father of one of my friends from Hamburg emigrated to the United States after 1870 rather than see himself integrated into the empire of Wilhelm I. It is the elites who make the world. And it is the strong who, with their boot on their behinds, push the weak forward. Without them the peoples, split up, would forever remain in their place.

In 1941 or in 1942, even if the victory of Hitler in Europe would have been total, irreversible, even if, as Spaak said, Germany would have been 'mistress of Europe for thousand years', the complainers would have multiplied in millions. Every person was attached to his hobby horse, to his corner of the country, superior, evidently, to all the other corners of the country! As a student I always heard with amazement my comrades of Charleroi shouting above their beer crates:

Country of Charleroi

It's you that I prefer!

The most beautiful corner of the earth,

Yes, it's you, it's you!

Now, it's the ugliest corner of the world, with its interminable terrace houses of blackish brick, under the hundred castles of its dusty waste-heaps! Even the flowers there are covered in coal!

---

63 tenaciously

However, with wondering eyes, the Charleroi boys bawled their enthusiasm! Everybody is besotted with his little village, his region, his kingdom, his republic.

But this European complex of the small and the mean could evolve, was even in the process of evolving. An accelerated evolution was not at all unrealisable.

The proof had been given, ten times, of the possibilities of unifying Europeans very distant from one another and who, however, are fundamentally the same. The hundred thousand French Protestants who had to leave their country after the revocation of the Edict of Nantes[64] amalgamated themselves marvellously with the Prussians who welcomed them. In the course of our combats of February and March 1945, in the villages of the east and west of the Oder, we saw everywhere, on signboards of peasant carts wonderful French names that evoked the territory of Anjou and Aquitaine.

At the front, von Dieu le Veut's, von Mezière's, de la Chevaleri's. Conversely, hundreds of thousands of German columns extended, in the course of several centuries, through the Baltic countries, in Hungary, in Romania, and even — hundred and fifty thousand! — along the Volga.

The Flemish, who came in very large numbers to the north of France, gave to the latter its most tenacious industrial elites. The benefits of these cohabitations have been evident also in the space termed Latin.

The Spanish of the Left, who had no other recourse than to seek refuge in France after their debacle of 1939, were mixed up with the French who welcomed them within one generation: a Maria Casarès, daughter of the prime minister of the Frente Popular, became one of the most admired actresses of the Théâtre-Français! The hundreds of thousands of Italians pushed to France by hunger during the last century were also assimilated with extreme ease.

---

64 The Edict of Nantes, which was signed in 1598 by Henri IV of France, granted the Calvinist Protestants (Huguenots) certain rights in the nation. It was revoked by Henri's grandson Louis XIV through the Edict of Fontainebleau, which subjected the French Protestants to persecution and forced them to flee from the country.

To such a degree that one of the greatest writers of France of the last century was the son of a Venitian: Zola. In our era, the writers who are sons of Italians are legion, with Giono[65] at their head.

The Napoleonic Empire also had collected the Europeans together without asking for their advice very much. However, one has read how their elites had joined one another with an extraordinary rapidity: The German Goethe was knight of the Legion of Honour; the Polish prince Poniatowski had become a French marshal; Goya provided the Louvre Museum with Spanish masters; Napoleon proclaimed himself, on his currency, Rex Italicus.

The old soldiers, recruited in ten different countries of Europe, had rubbed shoulders with one another, had fraternised, exactly as we did in our turn in the ranks of the Waffen SS during the Second World War. But every time, either persecution or war or the necessity of earning one's living, or the will of the strong man, had to give a helping hand. Normally the peoples of Europe clung to the little drainage canal of their borders. They went beyond it — and every time successfully — only when they were pushed out of it.

These fecund experiences, spread through time, unified the most diverse Europeans coming from Prussia as well as from Aquitaine, from Flanders as well as from Andalusia or Sicily, could perfectly well be repeated, accumulate and amplify themselves.

Won or lost, the Second World War was going to bring about the big beginning. It had obliged all the Europeans, and notably the adversaries who seemed the most irreducible, the French and the Germans, to rub shoulders with each other. Even if they detested each other, even if they only dreamed of kicking the other in the shins, they had to indeed learn, willingly or not, to get to know each other. These four years of fighting with each other, or of cohabiting for better or for worse, of seeking to understand each other, appreciating each other, were not in vain. Everybody had to confront each other, the victors and the vanquished. None would forget the face of the other. The bad moments would fade away.

---

65 Jean Giono (1895–1970) was a French novelist whose novels are often set in the Provence region.

One would remember, later, that which counts. The meeting of the European peoples had occurred.

During the twenty five years which have followed this meeting, other meetings have taken place according to the speed of our age. Dozens of millions of Europeans now travel. The foreigner is no longer a being that one looks at with fear or hatred, or with mockery. One mates with him. The man from Bresse no longer sees solely through his blue cheese and his ringed chickens. The Norman has gone beyond his cider works, and the Belgian his pot of Gueuze beer. Thousands of Swedish people live on the coast of Malaga. Michelin, in spite of its bicycle pliers, combines with the Italian Agnelli, and the German Gunther Sachs was able to marry a 'made in Paris' actress without the Republic collapsing.

Even General de Gaulle finds it good to reveal to the Frenchman that he has German blood in his veins, thanks to a grand-uncle who devoured sauerkraut, born in the country that rendered the Nazis so popular!

The young no longer even have a country, often. They feel denationalised. They have created their own world, of audacious or eccentric ideas, of frantic disks, of long hair, of frayed trousers, of loud shirts, of girls open broadly to the confusion of nationalities!

The little French cock of 1914 and the big black eagle gliding over the city have stopped emitting their cocorico's or shrieks. Their feathers, their beaks, their excrement and their gliding flight already appear, to the new generation, like strange prehistoric pieces for museums which will not even be visited.

This European, and even international, rapprochement, which has submerged centuries of the past in a quarter century, has operated without a political stimulant, except by circulating in millions from one country to another, looking at other landscapes and other faces in millions, at the cinema or on television. The customs have got mixed as naturally as the most diverse ingredients are mixed in a cocktail.

Under Hitler, certainly the process of unification would have developed even more rapidly and above all less anarchically.

A great common political construction would have directed and concentrated all the tendencies. First, millions of young people, non-German as well as German, who had fought together from the Vistula to the Volga, had become, in the efforts and sufferings experienced in common, comrades in life and death. They got to know one another. They appreciated one another.

The petty European rivalries of yesterday, hobby horses of backward bourgeois, appeared ridiculous. This 'we' was in 1945 only a kernel. But, in the centre of the biggest fruit is found a kernel, a principle. We were that kernel. Europe, a dough-like mass, had never borne it in itself. Now it existed. It contained already then the future.

A world to be created would be offered to all the youth by the Europe that emerged from genius and arms. The millions of young Europeans who remained indifferent during the war enjoying the stores of Papa and making an effort at blackmarketing were going to be tempted in their turn.

Instead of vegetating at Caudebec-en-Caux or at Wurstwezel, bent for fifty years over salted herrings or cheese-filled potatoes, millions of young people would have, displayed in front of their dynamic energy, the endless lands of the east offered to everybody, no matter if they were from Friesland, Lozère, Mecklenburg, or Abruzzo. There they could establish a true life as men, initiators, creators, leaders!

All of Europe would have been informed by this energetic current.

The ideal that had, in so few years, seized the hearts of all of the youth of the Third Reich, because it meant audacity, dedication, honour, projection towards the great, would have seized the hearts exactly in the same manner, the youth of all of Europe. The mediocre lives would be finished!

The always grey and shrunken horizon would be finished! Finished the life stuck to the same hamlet, the same grindstone, the same rack of the same mediocre residence, the basket of prejudices of relatives stablised in the small and the mouldy!

And if Hitler Had Won?

A vibrant world would hail the youth across thousands of kilometres without borders, where one could open one's lungs wide, have a voracious appetite, enjoy everything to the fullest, conquer everything in handfuls, with joy and faith!

The old people themselves would have followed finally, because money would have followed.

Instead of going round in bitter mumbling, dosages, stop-clocks stopped in order to prolong debates, the iron will of a leader and the decisions of responsible teams that would be installed to construct its works broadly would have, in twenty years, created a real Europe, not a hesitant congress of stooges eaten up by mistrust and hidden calculations, but a great political, social, economic unity without reserved areas.

One should have listened to Hitler expound, in his wooden shack, his great projects of the future! Gigantic canals would unite all the large European rivers, open to everybody's boats, from the Seine to the Volga, from the Vistula to the Danube. Double-decker trains — on the lower deck merchandise, above the passengers — on raised tracks, four metres wide, would conveniently cross the immense territories of the east where the former soldiers would have developed the most modern agricultural cultivation and industries in the world.

What do the few interminably discussed concentrations, limping on their wooden legs, which have been attempted under the aegis of the present Common Market, represent beside the great complexes that a real authority could implement — impose, if necessary — upon European economic forces that were upto now disparate, contradictory or hostile, stabbing each other in the back, doing double or triple work, selfish and anarchist? The firm hand of a master would have brought them back rapidly to the law of intellgent co-operation and the common interest.

The public during twenty years would have grumbled, baulked. But, after a generation, unity would have been realised. Europe would have constituted the biggest nursery of creative intelligence. The European masses would then have been able to breathe.

Discipline would have been able to relax once this battle of Europe was won.

Would Germany have devoured Europe ?

The danger did exist. Why deny it? The same danger had existed in the past. The France of

Napoleon would have been able to devour Europe. Personally, I do not think so. The diverse

European spirits, already under the Emperor, had been compensated.

The same ambition of domination laid in wait, indisputably, for Hitlerian Europe. The Germans are big eaters. Some of them considered Europe as their own meal. They were capable of numerous trip-ups through trickery. Of course, of course! We took that into consideration. We were afraid of that. If not, we would have been simpletons or, at the least, innocents, which is not worth much in politics. We took our precautions, seeking to seize, as firmly as possible, positions of control or of prestige whence we could defend ourselves, storm, or reduce the damages.

There were risks, that is of course true. It would be stupid to deny it. But there were also reasons of trust that were as strong.

Hitler, first, was a man used to seeing from afar, and whom German exceptionalism did not suffocate. He had been Austrian, and then German, then Greater German. From 1941, he had gone beyond all these stages, he was European. Genius soars above frontiers and races. Napoleon also was at first only a Corsican, and even an anti-French Corsican! Finally, at Sainte-Hélène, he spoke of the 'French people whom he had loved so much' as of an esteemed people but not his exclusively. What does the genius want? To go beyond himself always. The greater the mass that has to be moulded the more he is in his element. Napoleon in 1811 saw himself already arriving in India.

Europe, for Hitler, was a construction in his image. Germany was only an important building that he had constructed in the past, which he considered with pleasure. But he had already gone far beyond that. From his side no real danger existed of a Germanisation of Europe. It was the extreme opposite of everything that his ambition, his pride, his genius aimed at and dictated to him.

Were there other Germans? But there were also other Europeans! And these other Europeans possessed their own exceptional qualities indispensable to the Germans, without which their Europe would only be a heavy batter badly leavened. I think, especially, of the French genius. Never would the Germans have been able to bypass the genius of France in giving life to Europe, even if they had wanted not to have recourse to her, even if, as it was in the case of some people, they scorned it.

Nothing was possible and nothing will ever be possible in Europe without the French finesse and grace, without the vivacity and clarity of the French mind. The French people has the quickest intelligence. It captures, seizes, transports, transfigures. It is alive. It is light. The French taste is perfect. Never will one ever make a second cupola of the Invalides. Never will there be a second enchanting river like the eastern Loire. Never will there be a chic, a charm, a pleasure of living, as in Paris.

The Europe of Hitler would have been heavy in the beginning. Apart from a Goering, a Renaissance lord, who had a sense of art and splendour, a Goebbels with an intelligence sharp as a guillotine blade, a number of Hitlerian leaders were thick, vulgar like cowherds, without taste, delivering their doctrine, their ideas, their orders, like ground meat or bags of chemical fertilisers. But precisely because of this heaviness, the French genius would have been indispensable. In ten years it would have stamped everything. The Italian genius also would have formed a counterpoise to the too massive power of the Germans. One has often mocked the Italians. One has seen, since the war, what they were capable of. They would as easily have flooded a Hitlerian Europe as the narrow businesses of a novice Common Market with their impeccable shoes, their elegant fashion, their greyhound-like race cars.

The Russian genius would have equally intervened, I am sure, in a considerable manner in the refinement of an excessively German

Hitler for a 1000 Years

Europe, where two hundred million Slavs of the east would be integrated. Four years of living mixed with the Russian people made it esteemed, admired and loved by all the Soviet combatants. The misfortune is that for half a century the virtues of these two hundred million good people have been choked — and risk being that for a long time yet under the enormous iron slab of the regime of the Soviets.

These people are peaceful, intelligent and artistic, possessing also the gift of mathematics, which is not a contradiction: the law of numbers is the basis of all the arts.

While entering Russia the Germans, who had been subjected to a really summary Nazi indoctrination, imagined that the only valuable beings of the universe were the Aryans, who, necessarily, had to be blond giants, stocky like organ stops, whiter than tea, with blue eyes like the Tyrolian skies in August.

It was rather comical, for Hitler was not tall and had chestnut hair. Goebbels had one leg shorter than the other, he was short and dark as a prune. Zep Dietrich had the style of a stocky owner of a Marseilles bar. Bormann was twisted like a retired champion cyclist. Apart from some giants serving apéritifs on the terrace of Berchtesgaden, the big guys with bleached skin, blueberry eyes, were not abundant, one can see, in Hitler's entourage.

One may imagine the surprise of the Germans, hurtling towards Russia, at meeting only blond men with blue eyes, exact types of perfect Aryans that they had been made to admire exclusively! Blond men! Blond women! And what blonde women! Big farm girls, splendid, strong, wiht light blue eyes, more natural and healthy that everything that the Hitler Jugend had gathered together. One could not imagine a race more typically Aryan if one adhered to the sacrosant canons of Hitlerism!

In six months the entire German army had become Russophile. They fraternised everywhere with the peasants. And with the peasant women! As under Napoleon, Europe was made also in the embraces of European women, in this case these beautiful Russian women, built for love and fecundity, and whom one saw, during the retreat, follow desperately in the horror of the worst combats, the Erics, Walters, Karls, Wolfgangs, who had taught them, in the idle hours, that the pleasure of loving has its charm everywhere, even coming from the west.

Some Nazi theoreticians professed some violently anti-Slav theories. They would not have resisted ten years of Russo-Germanic cohabitation. The Russians of both sexes would have learnt German very fast. They already know it. We found German handbooks in all the schools. The link of language would have been established in Russia quicker than anywhere in Europe.

The German possesses admirable techical and organisational qualities. But the Russian, a dreamer, is more imaginative and has a more lively mind. One would have complemented the other. The links of blood would have done the rest. The young Germans quite naturally, and no matter what their propaganda would have done to oppose them, would have married hundreds of thousands of young Russians. They like them. The creation of eastern Europe would have been completed in the most pleasant manner. The Germano-Russian conjunction would have been a marvel.

Yes, the problem was gigantic: to weld five hundred million Europeans who did not have, to start with, any desire of coordinating their work, of combining their strengths, of harmonising their particular characters, their temperaments. But Hitler bore in himself the genius and the power capable of imposing and realising this gigantic work on which hundred politicians badly served by their mediocrity and their blinkers would have stumbled.

His million soldiers would have been there to second his peaceful action, coming from the whole of Europe, those of the Division Azul and those of the Baltic countries, those of the Division Flandern and those of the Balkans, those of the Division Charlemagne and their hundreds of thousands of comrades of the thirty eight divisions of the Waffen SS!

On the European peninsula which emerged in the west, after the deluge of the Third Reich, were built, nevertheless, the first counters, badly stocked, still not very stable, of a Common Market that is rather like a barter-house. Good. But a true Europe, raised by a heroic and revolutionary idea, built big, would have had quite another allure!

The life of the youth of all of Europe would have known another spirit and another sense than leading an existence of beatniks and protesters, rightly revolting against democratic regimes which do not offer them anything objective that could excite them, suffocating them on the contrary throughout the miserable post-war years.

After having revolted, the diverse European peoples would have been surprised to see that they complemented one another so well. The popular referendums would have confirmed, in our own lifetime, that the Europe of strength had become, from the Pyrenees to the Urals, *free Europe*, the Community of five hundred million like-minded Europeans. It is unfortunate that in the XIX century Napoleon failed. His Europe, based on the crucible of his epic, would have spared us many misfortunes, the two world wars especially. It would have in time, in his skilful hands, seized the big world-machine, instead of leaving Europe in its colonialist rivalries, often abject and greedy and which finally showed themselves to be unprofitable.

Similarly, it is unfortunate that in the XX century Hitler spoiled things in his turn. Communism would have been swept away. The United States would not have had the world bend under the dictatorship of consumerism. And, after twenty centuries of stuttering and failed efforts, the sons of five hundred million Europeans, united in spite of themselves in the beginning, would have finally possessed the most powerful political, social, economic and intellectual complex of the planet.

Would that have been a Europe of concentration camps?

So one is going to whistle this tune endlessly! As if there were nothing else but that that was edifying in Europe! As if, after the fall of Hitler, men had not continued to exterminate one another in Asia, America, Europe even, in the streets of Prague and Budapest!

As if the invasions, the violations of territories, the abuses of power, the plots, the political abductions, had not flourished, ever again, in Vietnam, in Saint-Domingue, in Venezuela, in the Bay of Pigs, in Cuba, including in Paris itself during the Ben Barka affair,[66] already forgotten! and even beyond the borders of Israel! Why not say that? For it is not Hitler, nevertheless, who rushed with his tanks towards Mount Sinai and occupied by force, in the Near East, the territories of others!

One should write — yes! — against violence, that is to say, more precisely against *all* violences. Not only against the violences of Hitler, but also against the violences of Mollet[67] throwing thousands of parachutists on the Suez Canal in 1956, with as much premeditation as deceit: against the violences of the Americans pelting the Vietnamese fifteen thousand kilometres from Massachusetts or Florida, whose lives they did not have to control in any way; against the violences of the English overwhelming the Nigerians with armies in order to free, thanks to a million dead Biafrans, the supercapitalist petrol wells; against the violences of the Soviets, flattening under their tanks the Hungarians and Czechs who refused their tyranny!

The same remark on the subject of war crimes.

They dragged the vanquished to Nuremberg, they imprisoned them like monkeys in little cells, they forbade their defence lawyer to make use of documents which could have disturbed the prosecutors, notably all reference to the massacre at Katyn of fifteen thousand Polish officers, because the representative of Stalin, their assassin, was part of the War Crimes Tribunal of Nuremberg instead of being brought before it. If on wishes to have recourse to such a procedure, let it be, of course, that it be valid for *all* criminals, not only the German criminals, but also for the English criminals who massacred two hundred thousand innocent people in Dresden, also for the French criminals who, without any judgement at all,

---

66 Mehdi Ben Barka (1920–?) was a socialist Moroccan politician who founded the Union Nationale des Forces Populaires which opposed French imperialism. In 1962 he was accused of plotting against King Hassan II and was exiled the next year. He 'disappeared' in Paris in 1965.
67 Guy Mollet (1905–1975) was Prime Minister of France from 1956 to 1957 during the Suez Crisis, when he joined forces with Great Britain and Israel against Nasser's attempt to nationalise the canal.

shot down on their territory defenceless German prisoners, also for the American criminals who crushed the sexual organs of the SS prisoners of Malmedy!

This procedure should be valid equally for the Soviet criminals who finished off the Second World War with frightful cruelties in occupied Europe and who burnt millions of people in their frightful concentration camps of the White Sea and Siberia.

Now those camps *have not been closed* since the Second World War like those of the Third Reich, on which, twenty years after their liquidation, they keep harping without respite. These camps of the USSR still exist today, and still function today. They continue to send today thousands of human beings who have the misfortune of displeasing Messrs. Brezhnev, Kosygin and other gentle democratic lambs! Of those camps, fully operational, where the Soviets implacably imprison all those who oppose their dictatorship, nobody breathes a word among the hecklers of the Left! None of them is offended by them!

Well then! Where is the desire for the truth? Equity? Where is the good faith? Where is the farce? Who is more repugnant? The one who kills? or the one who playacts in a drama about virtue and who is silent?

Seeing total impunity granted in this way to the criminal of peace time and of war as soon as they are not Germans, all the crooks of the post-war period have a field-day torturing to death, with an atrocious savagery, a Lumumba, killing a Che Guevara by machine-gun, assassinating with a revolver, in front of the press, prisoners in downtown Saigon, mounting with the most powerful accomplices, the public assassination — as at a shooting game in a fair — of a Kennedy I, then a Kennedy II, who disturbed in the USA the real power holders — the police and high finance, hiding under the democratic cover.

All the criminals in command! Whoever they may be! wherever they may be!

If not, so many virtuous shouts of indignant censors when it is a question of Hitler and dumb when it is no longer a question of him are only abject dramas, aiming only at converting the spirit of justice into a spirit of vengeance, and the criticism of violence into the most tortuous of hypocrisies!

Rest in peace those who died under Hitler! But the infernal agitation pursued incessantly on their urns by the false Puritans of democrary ends by becoming indecent! This scandalous blackmail has been pursued for more than twenty years, scandalous because it is conducted by a bias as total as cynical! The only meaning it has is for the small streets. History is not satisfied with it. It does not allow one to be converted into an alleyway where the provocateurs of eternal hatred, the white sepulchres, the falsifiers and impostors, are stationed watchfully.

An evaluation is an evaluation. In spite of the defeat in the USSR, in spite of the fact that Hitler was burnt, in spite of the fact that Mussolini was hanged, the 'fascisms' — along with the establishment of the Soviets in Russia — were the great event of the century.

Some of Hitler's preoccupations of 1930 have faded. The notion of living space has become outmoded. The proof — East Germany, reduced to a third of the territory of the greater Reich, is at present richer and more powerful than the Hitlerian state of 1939. The cheap international transports and maritime transports have changed everything. On a bald rock, well-located, one can at present establish the most powerful industry in the world.

The peasantry, so favoured by the 'fascisms', has everywhere been relegated to the second rank. An intelligently industrialised farm brings in more at present than hundred exploitations that are not rationalised and without modern, accurately adapted materials. A majority in the past, the peasants form an increasingly small minority.

Pasture and labour, dear already to Sully, have ceased to be the only nourishment of the peoples, either overfed or not having money to feed themselves. And, above all, the social doctrines, whatever they may have been, which took into account only capital and work have become outmoded.

A third element intervnes increasingly: grey matter. The economy is no longer a partnership of two people, but of three. A gram of creative intelligence is more important often than a train of coal or pyrite. The brain has become the raw material par excellence. A laboratory of scientific research can be more valuable than an assembly line. Before the capitalist and the worker is: the researcher!

Without him, without his highly specialised equipment, without his computers and his statistics, capital and work are lifeless bodies. The Krupps themselves and the Rothschilds have had to efface themselves before better constituted minds.

The development of these problems would not have caught Hitler off guard. He read everything, was well informed. His atomic laboratories were the first in the world. The characteristic of genius is that it is incessantly recycled. Hitler, an imaginative furnace in continual combustion, would have foreseen every event and change.

He had, above all, formed *men*.

Germany and Italy, though defeated, crushed (the Third Reich was no more than a fabulous heap of debris and bricks in 1945), did not waste time in becoming the leaders of Europe. Why? Because the great school of Hitlerism and Fascism had created *characters*. It had formed thousands of young leaders, had given a *personality* to thousands of beings, had revealed to them, in exceptional circumstances, gifts of organisation and command that the stupid little semi-bourgois routine of the preceding times would never have allowed them to display.

The German miracle after 1945 was that: a generation, materially crushed, had been prepared in a superior manner for a role of leaders by a doctrine based on authority, on responsibility, on the spirit of initiative; through a baptism of fire the latter had given to the characters the moral fibre of the best quality which, at the moment when it was necessary to reconstruct everything, showed itself to be an irresistible lever. But Germany and Italy were not the only ones to be raised by the great Hitlerian hurricane. Our century

And if Hitler Had Won?

has been shaken by him to its very foundations, transformed in all its fields, whether it is a question of the state, of social relations, the economy or scientific research.

The present deployment of modern discoveries, from nuclear energy to miniaturisation, it is Hitler — close your ears, but it is so! — who set it in motion, when a dozing Europe ate its daily soup without worrying about seeing farther than its bowl.

What would a von Braun, a massive young German, totally unknown and without resources, be without Hitler? During the difficult years, the latter pushed him, motivated him. Goebbels sometimes took over, supporting von Braun with his friendship. Even in 1944 this minister — the most intelligent of Hitler's ministers — left his work to encourage von Braun with his friendship.

This was the case with hundreds of others. They had talent. But what would they have done with their talent alone?

The Americans knew well that the scientific future of the world was there, in Hitler's laboratories. While they allowed themselves complacently to be presented as the kings of science and technology, they did not have a greater concern, when they were victors in May 1945, than to rush through the Third Reich, still smoking, to recuperate hundreds of nuclear scientists.

The Soviets ran a parallel race. They transported Hitler's scientists to Moscow in train-loads.

To all of those among them that it could find America offered golden bridges. The USA took as the director of their immense nuclear complex the von Braun of Hitler, to whom modern America owes so much for it was he who in August 1939, thus even before the Second World War began, was the first to fire the first rocket in the world into the skies of Prussia.

The modern world was born on that day.

Just as gunpowder, which killed, has served the world, the nuclear era, inaugurated by Hitler in 1939, will transform the future centuries. There too, as in the social field, the denigrators of Hitler are only late imitators. Is the Centre de Recherches of Pierrelatte anything else but a version of the Hitlerian base of Peenemünde twenty five years later?

Hitler has disappeared, the democratic world has shown itself incapable of creating anything new in the political and social fields, or even of patching up things with old.

It has tried in vain to raise up again the old emaciated horses of the pre-war, they have fallen on the ground muddied.

From Nasser to de Gaulle, from Tito to Castro, wherever one looks, among the old countries which attempt to emerge from the past or among the new countries of the Third World that are awakening, everywhere the formulas — nationalism and socialism, resurge, represented by a strong man, incarnation and guide of the people, a powerful magnet of wills, a creator of ideals and faith.

The democratic myth, of the old style, fireman-like, garrulous, incompetent, sterile, is only a balloon with hundred empty heads, who does not mystify anybody any more, does not interest anybody any more, and even makes the young laugh.

Who is still preoccupied with old parties and their old discredited and forgotten phonies? But Hitler, Mussolini, who will ever forget them? . . . Millions of our boys are dead, after a horrible odyssey. What has become of their poor tombs there? . . . Our own lives, those of the survivors, have been ground, pillaged, definitively eliminated. But the fascisms for which we lived have modelled our epoch forever. In our misfortunes it is our great joy.

They will tatoo our soldiers' arms in vain! Too late! We look at the exterminators defying them. The curtain of history can fall on Hitler and Mussolini, as it fell on Napoleon. The dwarfs will not change anything. The great revolution of the XX century has already taken place.

Select Bibliography

Léon Degrelle's post-war writings

La Cohue de 1940, R. Crausaz, 1949

La Campagne de Russie, 1941-1945, Le Cheval Ailé, 1949

(English edition: *Campaign in Russia: The Waffen SS on the Eastern Front*, IHR, 1985)

Les Âmes qui brulent, À la feuille de Chêne, 1964

Front de l'est, 1941-1945 (revised edition of *La Campagne de Russie*), La Table Ronde, 1969

(English edition: *The Eastern Front: Memoirs of a Waffen SS Volunteer 1941-1945*, IHR, 1985)

Hitler pour mille ans, Paris, La Table Ronde, 1969

Lettre à Jean-Paul II à propos de Auschwitz, l'Europe Réelle, 1979

Appel aux jeunes européens, Avalon, 1992

Lettre à mon cardinal, l'Europe Réelle, 1975

Mon chemin de Saint Jacques, l'Homme Libre, 2002

Le fascinant Hitler!, l'Étoile mystérieuse, 2006

Le Siècle de Hitler, 1986–

Vol.1: Hitler né à Versailles (Art et Histoire de l'Europe, 1986–88)

   i — Le traquenard de Sarajevo

   ii — La pseudo-guerre du droit 1914-1918

   iii — Les tricheurs de Versailles

Vol.2: Le Hitler de la paix (l'Homme Libre, 2002-2006)

i — Hitler démocrate (English edition, *Hitler Democrat*, Barnes Review, 2012)

ii — Hitler, unificateur des Allemands

CPSIA information can be obtained
at www.ICGtesting.com
Printed in the USA
FFHW010858180719
53607179-59289FF